TRUE AND TALL TALES OF THE GLORY DAYS

Told by MUSICIANS, DJs, PROMOTERS & FANS

Who Made the Scene in the ’60s, ’70s, and ’80s

CARLO WOLFF

GRAY & COMPANY, PUBLISHERS
CLEVELAND

Photo credits appear on page 130.

Gray & Company, Publishers
www.grayco.com

Library of Congress Cataloging-in-Publication Data
Wolff, Carlo.
Cleveland rock and roll memories : true and tall tales of the glory days, told by musicians, DJs, promoters, and fans who made the scene / by Carlo Wolff.
p. cm.
ISBN: 978-1-886228-99-3 (pbk.)
1. Rock music—Ohio—Cleveland—History and criticism. I. Title.
ML3534.W616 2006
781.6609771'32—dc22 2006031216

Printed in the United States of America

CONTENTS

FOREWORD by Daffy Dan Gray

Many a book has been written about Cleveland rock and roll, chronicling it from its birth more than a half century ago. For a Cleveland rock and roll fan, those books have been great trips down memory lane. In this book, *Cleveland Rock and Roll Memories,* Carlo Wolff adds his encouragement to keep on rockin'.

Carlo has let those who played the music, filled the airwaves with it, sold it, staged concerts, established venues for it, promoted the lifestyle, and all of us fans tell the story in our own words. He seems to have talked with just about everyone for these reminiscences and celebrations.

Cleveland musicians have an annual picnic where they share memories. Record industry people, retailers, distribution-level folk, and those infamous promotion people and salesmen used to meet once a month; they still do at holiday time. On-air radio personalities, engineers, sales and marketing people, past interns, anybody who walked through radio station doors—they still get together for birthdays, milestones, or just at the drop of a hat. And who could overlook one of the best-known storytelling events—the legendary annual Taurus parties! There are, I'm sure, dozens of other reunions and gatherings.

The fans—all of us, and I do mean all of us—share memories every chance we get, whether at a bar, a party, the office, or with the person standing beside us at the bus stop. Almost every man, woman, and child living in this city has been affected by the unique phenomenon of Cleveland rock and roll.

It's as if the stars lined up just right to make Cleveland the place where rock history was to be created. Other cities may lay claim to their own rock experience, but in no other city have so many for so long shared something so special as what we have had in Cleveland. Starting with WHK, then WIXY—then the piece de resistance, WMMS—Cleveland rock and roll was a totally shared lifestyle experience.

The music wrapped around us like a blanket, a blanket in which all of us were threads woven together to create the fabric of this thing we call Cleveland rock and roll. The clubs, the promoters, the musicians, the DJs and radio personalities, the record companies and promo people, the record stores, the "lifestyle" purveyors, and most importantly, the fans, like you and me, have all been drivers and passengers on this magical, musical bus.

I personally was able to build a life out of T-shirts and rock and roll—twenty-seven stores based solely on selling Agora concert tickets and putting "uniforms" on the backs of the Buzzard Army. Daffy Dan's sold millions upon millions of WMMS T-shirts, jerseys, jackets, caps, scarves, mugs, jugs, belt buckles, you name it—everything that made listeners feel they were part of the Cleveland rock and roll movement. Recruiting that "army" created a loyalty to WMMS unrivaled by any other station in the country. We still get calls every day for vintage WMMS shirts.

My own stories are endless, as they are endless for every Cleveland rock and roll fan. Carlo could have put together a book ten, a hundred, a thousand times thicker than this, and still he would have collected only a small sample of the memories that make up the fabric of Cleveland rock. Read and enjoy, my fellow rock and roll fans. Let's all keep the rock rolling in Cleveland.

—Daffy Dan Gray

WHY CLEVELAND ROCKS—AND HOW!

Writing about rock and roll in Cleveland feels like destiny for me.

I'd been writing about rock for *Billboard* magazine for a few years when I moved here from upstate New York in 1986. I was eager to write about rock in a big city, particularly with the rock hall on the horizon. The first Cleveland band I reviewed was Pere Ubu in 1978 when they played the Hullabaloo in Rensselaer, New York. Ubu was great; I'd never heard anything like it and it gave me a lasting taste for Cleveland music. I wanted to find out how one city could produce both Ubu and the Raspberries, a great group of a very different kind.

When I moved to Cleveland, the rock hall was beginning to gather steam and the scene was lively. The first local show I reviewed was Ratt at the Coliseum. I wrote about all kinds of shows for the *Plain Dealer* and the *Akron Beacon Journal*. Covering George Michael on his "Faith" tour was fascinating. So was rocking to Joan Jett when she played here behind the *Light of Day* movie.

Cleveland had cool record stores and comfortable venues. I went to Peabody's a lot, the Phantasy, Music Hall, Public Hall, Nautica (Nine Inch Nails playing Joy Division's "Dead Souls" while a freighter passed behind the stage was thrilling), and Blossom. I sweated as hard as the walls when Megadeth threatened to blow out the Phantasy. I levitated with Moby one summer night in 1995 at Peabody's. I wrote about the business, too, and made many of the connections that shaped this book.

No way can I include everything or everybody here. This is not meant to be an encyclopedia. It's not conventional history, either. It's nostalgia, a book by, for, and about fans. I've tried to communicate the texture of Cleveland rock, remind people why rock shows here are so special. It's because Cleveland has an unusual appetite for rock and roll.

I've been going to shows since the '60s. I saw Howlin' Wolf at Club 47 in Cambridge, Massachusetts. I heard Marc Bolan and Peregrin Took, those pixyish folk who called themselves Tyrannosaurus Rex, at a free concert in Cambridge. I saw the Doors in a suburban Boston bar, Little Feat at Pall's Mall on Boylston Street. I blew my ears out to the Hallucinations, the band that predated J. Geils. I was tripping, so I didn't care how loud it was next to the speakers.

The first band I ever reviewed was Edgar Winter's White Trash, in Burlington, Vermont, in 1971. It was the first rock review ever printed in the *Burlington Free Press*. I felt like a pioneer. Hell, I was a pioneer. Young, too, like rock.

My first link to Cleveland and Cleveland rock was in 1965 when a friend and I hitched from Boston to California. We arrived in Cleveland at night and two blond longhairs in a GTO picked us up and drove us through town fast, Grand Funk blaring over their AM radio.

It would be years before I made Cleveland my home. In Burlington, I reviewed Mountain opening for Traffic, Springsteen behind *The Wild, the Innocent and the E Street Shuffle*. When I lived in Albany, New York, in the '70s and '80s, I reviewed everybody from Liberace to Iggy Pop. I really liked new wave; I really like good pop. I interviewed U2 when they were babies and wrote that Pat Benatar was a flash in the pan (wrong).

But when I got to Cleveland, rock and my writing found a whole new dimension.

I have vivid memories of Cleveland rock, like pumping my fists with my buddy Dan Cook during a Def Leppard concert at the Coliseum in 1994 (we were the old guys for sure) or dancing in the aisles at Cain Park in 1998 at the Brian Setzer Orchestra Tiki lounge extravaganza. "Cleveland rocks" may be a cliché, but clichés are clichés because they're true. Putting this together was a blast. Read it and rock all over again.

CROSSING OVER: That's Alan Freed of WJW running a record hop in the early '50s. He clearly struck a chord among black teen-agers—and whites eager to groove to rock and roll, too.

MAKING WAVES

Radio

One reason rock and roll is synonymous with Cleveland is radio and the personalities that gave it such character. From WJW, WERE, and WIXY in the AM area to WMMS in the glory days of FM, Cleveland radio has meant rock.

In the late '40s and early '50s, when radio was much more segregated than today, there were "race" stations and white stations.

In the black community, rhythm 'n' blues, the then-new name for "race music," was the rage. Rhyming disc jockey Bill Hawkins, the first black DJ in town, was the man.

"Walkin', Talkin' Bill Hawkins used to broadcast out of a window on 105th from Hawkins Music Stop," said John Lenear, vice president of advertising at the *Call & Post,* Cleveland. (Lenear died July 14, 2006.)

Hawkins's store was part of a thriving scene along East 105th Street between Cedar Road and Euclid Avenue. "Cedar was a community, there was a drugstore on the corner where we used to get milkshakes, you could buy ice cream hand packed."

Lenear recalled Hawkins as a tall, mustachioed man who played rhythm 'n' blues over WHK. "That's the only music there was. There was no rock and roll. The white music then consisted of Frank Sinatra and Dean Martin, and Johnnie Ray was, what kind of freak is this? Bill Randle, for black artists, I think he played Roy Hamilton, Johnny Nash, the Platters, Johnny Mathis—the white stuff."

Hawkins was Alan Freed's biggest competitor for the ear of the black audience, said Lenear, who worked for Freed and occasionally sang with the Five Quails, a doo-wop group.

Dick Goddard met Freed, the famous DJ best known as Moondog, in the late '40s, when Goddard was a football player at Greensburg High School and Freed was a DJ at WAKR in Akron.

THE PRINCE OF PLAID: **Alan Freed sure looked good on radio.**

BLASTING OFF: **Cut short when the crowd lost control, Alan Freed's Moondog Coronation Ball launched the rock and roll era.**

> He played what was current back then, and the lyrics were not outrageous—they were very danceable and listenable, and you actually had melodies to songs, something that has long ago disappeared. —**Dick Goddard, TV personality**

By the time Freed began broadcasting over WJW in 1951, he'd befriended Leo Mintz, owner of Record Rendezvous on Prospect, and had begun playing black music for white kids. Some credit him, some Mintz, for coining the term "rock and roll." Some, like WIXY founder Norman Wain, suggest Freed was at his strongest in Cleveland. He certainly made a huge mark here, mounting the Moondog Coronation Ball at the Cleveland Arena on March 21, 1952. Billed as the first rock and roll concert, it created bedlam when sixteen to twenty-five thousand tickets were sold for a venue that seated only ten thousand.

> Freed had already done that Moondog thing at the Arena not too long before. Alan Freed was a master of the theater of the mind: He had that sound, that little castanet sound from that Moondog beggar in New York, the show would start with that ch ch chchchchch, then you'd hear that howl. He comes on and says, "Down boy, down, we're going to rock tonight." He adopted what the black jocks did, he'd talk right through the records, he'd urge the singers on, he talked over almost every record. About a year later in New York, I was listening to WINS [where Freed ended up], it was terrible, he didn't do any of the imaginative, exciting things that made that show. —**Norman Wain, WIXY co-founder**

Notable Cleveland Rock and Roll DJs of the 1950s

Scott Burton, WHK
Tommy Edwards, WERE
Joe Finan, KYW
Alan Freed, WJW
Bill Hawkins, WJMO
Wes Hopkins, KYW
Specs Howard, KYW
Phil McLean, WERE
Pete "Mad Daddy" Myers, WJW, WHK
Bill Randle, WERE
Carl Reese, WERE
Sam Sampson, WSRS, WJW
"Jockey" John Slade, WJMO
Norman Wain, WDOK

"Down boy, down, we're going to rock tonight."

No one downplays the importance of the Moondog Coronation Ball or of Freed's role in rock. Some credit Freed and Mintz with coining the term "rock and roll." But some were familiar with the term before it became a musical tag, like the man who brought us the Agora:

> I heard rock and roll before it was coined into music. I remember at one bar this guy was yelling at this girl, "c'mon, baby, let's rock and roll." He meant let's go to bed and make love. That had to be '49 or '50, the first time I heard that term "rock and roll." It was part of their language. Rock and roll meant "let's go to bed." —**Hank LoConti, founder of the Agora**

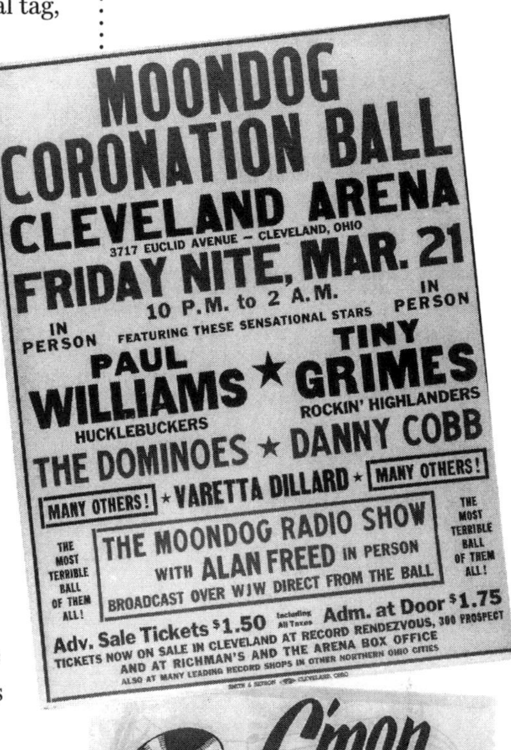

It was a black and white world indeed. Lenear recalled: "We did an event where we opened up a show for Bill Randle at some West Side high school, an all-white high school; the only black thing out there was the five of us. It was in a big gym and all the girls had on plaid skirts and white socks rolled up."

Randle, who died in January 2004 at eighty-one, was one of the most influential disc jockeys of the '50s and '60s. Critical to the career of Presley, he also "broke" artists such as Bobby Darin, Tony Bennett, and the wild crooner Johnnie Ray. Besides his work in the music industry, he was a teacher and a lawyer.

Rock was just beginning; there were no huge concerts, no clubs for kids, and in the late '40s and early '50s, the hits were mainstream, by Nat "King" Cole, Frank Sinatra, and, thanks to Randle, Johnnie Ray.

> When the white artists started coming, they weren't going to sing rhythm 'n' blues. So they changed it to rock and roll. Billy Ward and the Dominoes, the Ravens, the Swallows, those smooth groups, that's who you patterned yourself after. You sang sweet stuff. Bill Haley and the Comets finally came in with a backbeat. Alan Freed was the big dog. He helped folks who wanted to record, because he's responsible for the Moonglows, Harvey Fuqua and those guys. Harvey was our manager. Alan Freed played a lot of our stuff because Harvey made sure that we got plenty of airplay. That was in the days when you dropped $100 on the table, you got some airtime.
> —**Bill Strawbridge, musician**

They used to do a lot of record hops back in those days, with Carl Reese from WERE. In those days, the talent, like Carl, didn't touch any equipment. They had an engineer in the control room who played all the records, did all the commercials, kept a log. I remember doing a YMCA down around Five Points in East Cleveland. The DJ would spin records for a certain portion of the night, then they would have an additional attraction, the live band. There were generally a lot of people there because Carl was a high-profile disc jockey. —**George Stage, fan (Kirtland)**

The DJs with the highest profile were Freed and Randle. Freed, of course, is best known—in Cleveland, at least—for the Moondog Coronation Ball. Randle is famous for breaking Elvis Presley north of the Mason-Dixon Line and for having a golden ear.

I go back to '54 and '55 when I was in a children's home, monopolizing Bill Randle on WERE. By '55, he was playing "Heartbreak Hotel" and "Mystery Train," and Fats Domino; he pushed Fats. He didn't push Little Richard; Richard was a little wild for Bill's tastes.
—**Bill Miller, musician (Mr. Stress Blues Band)**

The first time Presley played Cleveland was February 26, 1955, at the Circle Theater. He returned there on October 19, when WERE-AM DJs Tommy Edwards and Randle brought him to play the venue at East 105th and Euclid. The following night, Randle presented the Hillbilly Cat at Brooklyn High School. Pat Boone, a Randle project, was also on the bill. On January 28, 1956, Randle introduced Presley to national television on *The Jackie Gleason Show*.

HERE'S TALKIN' TO YA: Pat Randle falls under dad Bill's spell at AM powerhouse WERE.

In 1954 there were eight AM radio stations and Randle had 50 percent of the audience. I had a show from 2 to 7 and at 6:30 I used to do "Big Chief's Mambo Matinee" and play Latin records. Randle was at 1300 at WERE, I was at 1260, and at 6:30 every night he'd play a Latin song to confuse the audience so if you were tuning in you might think it was him. When record pluggers used to come and visit, I would ask why. They confessed it was a way to maybe force Randle to play a record.

Randle was the most incredible person I've ever met in my life; he had an IQ—must have been 180. He had a photographic mind and an absolutely perfect memory. He invented the whole idea of music research; he had his mother in Detroit, some friends in Pittsburgh, and lots of spies in the Cleveland area checking up on store sales, and the minute anything started breaking, he would get behind it. He wasn't always first but he made you think he was first. I remember playing a record for fourteen days, the record's beginning to sell, Randle would play it and say, "You heard it first on *The Bill Randle Show*."

One time, I think it was '55, Randle gets ahold of me, says, "Come on, we're going to see the next big name in American music. This is his first concert above the Mason-Dixon Line," and in walks this little skinny kid and he starts shaking his hips with three guys behind him—his name was Elvis Presley. I said, "You got to be out of your mind." Bill says to me, "Remember the name Elvis Presley." I couldn't even spell it. Bill said, "I've been tracking him since his first recordings at Sun Records in Memphis."

He would play rock records back to back with something from the Mormon Tabernacle Choir. He only liked the specific record, and he liked anything that was happening. He went wherever the audience pulled him. **—Norman Wain**

ELVISMANIA:

Elvis Presley and Bill Black (to his right) drive the girls wild at Brooklyn High School. WERE-AM DJs Bill Randle (far left) and Tommy Edwards keep the kids at bay.

"In walks this little skinny kid and he starts shaking his hips with three guys behind him."

You could never figure what the guy was going to do. He had so much money and connections and stuff, he had 50 million college degrees, and he used to consistently brag. God, did he brag. He was always telling you about he did this, and he did that. He did accomplish a lot, I guess.

—Harvey Pekar, graphic novelist, music critic

Randle soldiered on into the 1990s; Freed, meanwhile, worked for WJW until 1954, when he left for New York's AM powerhouse, WINS. In 1959, the payola scandal, targeting disc jockeys who traded pay for record play, broke—and broke Freed. Other Cleveland DJs probed for accepting gifts and money to promote records included KYW's Joe Finan and Wes Hopkins. Top 40 radio was about to hit. Its standard bearers in the Cleveland area were KYW, CKLW—and WIXY.

CKLW was big, out of Detroit, it was where all the Motown came from. It's actually in Windsor, and because of federal laws in Canada, it had to

one*** 1 ***share

JERRY G & CO.
STOCK

WKYC RADIO 1100

No. 7974

THIS CERTIFIES THAT: Janet Macoska

being of Sound mind and radio listening habits is the owner of –ONE– share of pretty common stock of:
JERRY G & CO.
a corporate disorganization founded upon the highest principles of fun and nonsense. Actual cash value of this stock is guaranteed not to exceed the value of the paper upon which it is printed!

In witness whereof I hereby affix my signature:

Jerry G.
Founder, President, Head Cheerleader and Chairman of the Bored

Phil Music
director-in-chief

Zelda Goldfarb
secretary

MOHAIR AND MOTOWN:

KYW and WKYC's Jerry G worked sock hops and airwaves with style and sass.

MIXING IT UP ON TOP 40:

This WIXY playlist shows how rich rock was in the late '60s, with Motown, British Invasion, homegrown, pop and soul vying for dominance.

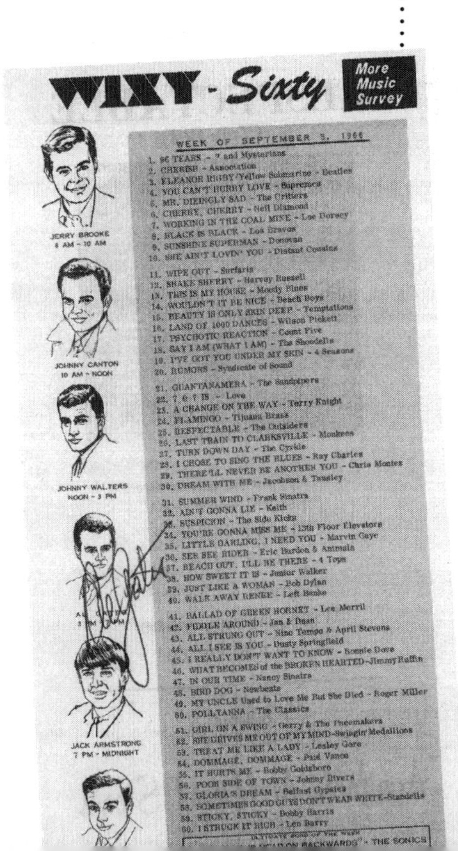

WIXY - Sixty

More Music Survey

WEEK OF SEPTEMBER 5, 1966

1. 96 TEARS - ? and Mysterians
2. CHERISH - Association
3. ELEANOR RIGBY/Yellow Submarine - Beatles
4. YOU CAN'T HURRY LOVE - Supremes
5. MR. DIEINGLY SAD - The Critters
6. CHERRY, CHERRY - Neil Diamond
7. WORKING IN THE COAL MINE - Lee Dorsey
8. BLACK IS BLACK - Los Bravos
9. SUNSHINE SUPERMAN - Donovan
10. SHE AIN'T LOVIN' YOU - Distant Cousins
11. WIPE OUT - Surfaris
12. SHAKE SHERRY - Harvey Russell
13. THIS IS MY HOUSE - Moody Blues
14. WOULDN'T IT BE NICE - Beach Boys
15. BEAUTY IS ONLY SKIN DEEP - Temptations
16. LAND OF 1000 DANCES - Wilson Pickett
17. PSYCHOTIC REACTION - Count Five
18. SAY I AM (WHAT I AM) - The Shondells
19. I'VE GOT YOU UNDER MY SKIN - 4 Seasons
20. RUMORS - Syndicate of Sound
21. GUANTANAMERA - The Sandpipers
22. 7 & 7 IS - Love
23. A CHANGE ON THE WAY - Terry Knight
24. FLAMINGO - Tijuana Brass
25. RESPECTABLE - The Outsiders
26. LAST TRAIN TO CLARKSVILLE - Monkees
27. TURN DOWN DAY - The Cyrkle
28. I CHOSE TO SING THE BLUES - Ray Charles
29. THERE'LL NEVER BE ANOTHER YOU - Chris Montez
30. DREAM WITH ME - Jacobson & Tausley
31. SUMMER WIND - Frank Sinatra
32. AIN'T GONNA LIE - Keith
33. SUSPICION - The Side Kicks
34. YOU'RE GONNA MISS ME - 13th Floor Elevators
35. LITTLE DARLING, I NEED YOU - Marvin Gaye
36. SEE SEE RIDER - Eric Burdon & Animals
37. REACH OUT, I'LL BE THERE - 4 Tops
38. HOW SWEET IT IS - Junior Walker
39. JUST LIKE A WOMAN - Bob Dylan
40. WALK AWAY RENEE - Left Banke
41. BALLAD OF GREEN HORNET - Lee Merril
42. FIDDLE AROUND - Jan & Dean
43. ALL STRUNG OUT - Nino Tempo & April Stevens
44. ALL I SEE IS YOU - Dusty Springfield
45. I REALLY DON'T WANT TO KNOW - Ronnie Dove
46. WHAT BECOMES of the BROKEN HEARTED - Jimmy Ruffin
47. IN OUR TIME - Nancy Sinatra
48. BIRD DOG - Newbeats
49. MY UNCLE Used to Love Me But She Died - Roger Miller
50. POLLYANNA - The Classics
51. GIRL ON A SWING - Gerry & The Pacemakers
52. SHE DRIVES ME OUT OF MY MIND - Swingin' Medallions
53. TREAT ME LIKE A LADY - Lesley Gore
54. DOMMAGE, DOMMAGE - Paul Vance
55. IT HURTS ME - Bobby Goldsboro
56. POOR SIDE OF TOWN - Johnny Rivers
57. GLORIA'S DREAM - Belfast Gypsies
58. SOMETIMES GOOD GUYS DON'T WEAR WHITE - Standells
59. STICKY, STICKY - Bobby Harris
60. I STRUCK IT RICH - Len Barry

"... ON BACKWARDS" - THE SONICS

play a certain amount of Canadian music, so the Guess Who and Gordon Lightfoot came out of there first. A lot of big artists became really big in Cleveland because of CKLW: the Rationals, Ted Nugent, they were out of Detroit; Mitch Ryder, Terry Knight and the Pack. —**Greg Beaumont, owner of the Record Den in Mentor**

Perhaps the Detroit–Cleveland connection explains why Terry Knight and the Pack, which would evolve into Grand Funk Railroad, became the first rock group to play La Cave—that basement club off University Circle where folk turned into rock—on September 27, 1966.

I liked CKLW a lot more than WIXY. The disc jockeys made it seem exciting; they may have been a little more cutting-edge than the Cleveland stations. The power chords really got me the first time, like on "She's Not There," by the Zombies. They'd play "Empty Heart" by the Rolling Stones, an album cut on "12 x 5," and the disc jockey would play it three or four times in a row because he couldn't get enough of it. —**Denny Carleton, musician (Lost Souls, The Choir)**

We ended up listening to radio like crazy: KYW, WHK, WIXY. There was a disc jockey on CKLW named Shannon and he said the sun never sets on the Shannon empire. He sounded so British, and they were playing the British groups. When I go back now and look at some of the playlists, it wasn't just British bands like I remember. Radio was our link to each other . . . Wherever you were you had your transistor radio. I can't remember being without a transistor radio once I got into junior high. Before I had a car, I had a transistor radio taped to the handlebars of my bike. When we got together, it was "Did you hear this record? Did you hear that? Did you hear this? —**John Awarski, fan (Cleveland)**

"Before I had a car, I had a transistor radio taped to the handlebars of my bike."

Thanks to my older brother and sister I was exposed to the hit parade in the '50s and '60s via radio, primarily and initially (as I can remember) WHK Color Radio and the good guys, especially Johnny Holliday. Then it was WIXY 1260 and CKLW the Big 8 in Detroit. Those pretty much saw me through the '60s, although I lost interest in radio around '68–'69 and pretty much listened to records for a while until WMMS radio entered my life via a homemade FM tuner. —**Matt "the Cat" Lapczynski, former WMMS DJ**

By the late '60s, WIXY was the top AMer. Founded in 1965 by Bob Weiss, Norman Wain, and Joe Zingale, the station locked into a groove in 1966, when Larry Morrow joined from CKLW, a 50,000-watter at 800 AM; WIXY was only 5,000 watts, out of Seven Hills. To pump it up, Wain needed Morrow, aka the Duker.

Morrow had his first interview in Cleveland, on July 23, 1966, the last of six days of the Hough riots:

> I turned on the television, I saw a movie on that I didn't want to see, which actually was the Hough riots. It had a bunch of army national guardsmen fighting with the police; then I turned to Channel 5 and said, that's unusual to have the same movie on both channels. Then I went to Channel 8 and realized what was going on. It was scary . . . I needed the job, and I couldn't work in Detroit because CKLW owned the name Duke Windsor, and I was popular in Detroit. The radio stations didn't want to hear about Larry Morrow; they wanted Duke Windsor.
>
> Norm Wain was out of town when I started on September 23 and maybe three or four days before, Jane Scott had done an interview. In the interview, she said, "What are they going to call you?" I said I think I'm going to use my real name, Larry Morrow. So she writes, "WIXY Makes the Duker Theirs," but she talks about Larry Morrow. Norm Wain is driving back from Pittsburgh and when he picks up his radio station to hear his new guy, Duke Windsor, he hears Larry Morrow and is livid. He runs in the radio station and says, "I hired Duke Windsor." No one knows who the hell Larry Morrow is. I said, "Hey, I've been on the air for a week already as Larry the Duker Morrow." The Duker it was. —**Larry Morrow, radio personality**

WIXY's glory days were 1966 to 1971, when Wain and his associates sold it. The station stayed in operation until 1975. Among its celebrities: Morrow, Armstrong, Mike Reineri, Dick "Wilde Childe" Kemp, Lou "King" Kirby, Jerry Brooke, Bobby Magic—and, briefly, Billy Bass. It was the WMMS of its day: high profile, promotionally brilliant, community oriented, marketing driven. It had a whole gang of personality:

TAKING IT TO THE STREETS:

WIXY's mobile studio brought the city's most popular jocks to the fans while broadcasting from special events.

AN ALL-STAR WIXY LINEUP:

This free concert drew around 100,000, and even rain refused to dampen the crowd's spirit.

First of all, the music was very exciting in those days. The Beatles were coming out with their stuff. Elvis Presley was hot. All the records were fantastic; they were all short and exciting. On top of that, we threw every possible promotion you could think of into the mix. One of the biggest things we ever did was the Francine contest, where this girl with big boobs was attracting all the attention on Wall Street—we tried to find a Cleveland girl who could do that, we found two and sent them to New York. We had all kinds of ticket giveaways. There was a song, "Lady Godiva" [by Peter and Gordon, 1966], so we put this woman who looked like she was naked on a horse and rode her down Euclid Avenue. We had the WIXY 1260 Superstars; the jocks went out and played basketball against high school teams. It wasn't just the music, the jocks were wild, and there was so much going on we knew we were the talk of the town and if you didn't listen, you missed a day, you missed a lot. —**Norman Wain, WIXY co-founder**

Larry Morrow drove Neil Diamond and his band to Chippewa Lake for a concert in August 1968 in "our first annual WIXY Appreciation Day."

Neil Diamond had a song out called "Solitary Man." I picked Neil Diamond up at the airport with his band in my new Chevy wagon. They had their instruments; I picked up the drums. There were four of them, and I brought them to the concert and took them back. The second year we moved it to Geauga Lake. It was outdoors, all outdoors, right by the water.

SOLITARY MAN? HARDLY:

Neil Diamond had a lot of company at the first WIXY Appreciation Day.

"We didn't pay anybody. In those days, they came in to promote their records."

A hundred thousand came. Unbelievable. It was free. We did two or three of them. I remember Tommy James and the Shondells were there; Smokey Robinson and the Miracles came in. We didn't pay anybody. In those days, they came in to promote their records, and WIXY 1260 was just starting to become recognized nationally as a station where you could break records. And Cleveland, Ohio, was a great city to break records. —**Larry Morrow**

GOING TO THE LIMIT: **Pioneering DJ Martin Perlich spins a platter on his show, "The Perlich Project." It was the dawn of underground radio.**

FM was beginning to rear its head, however. Shaker Heights native Martin Perlich, a pioneer of so-called free-form radio with his Perlich Project, reminisces:

> The rock scene in '62 would have meant Brian Hyland, the Four Seasons, Dion and the Belmonts . . . to me, if you didn't listen to Bartok and Alban Berg you listened to Thelonious Monk and John Coltrane. I was an improvising pianist, rock and roll to me was baby music, and it had no adult content and was purely a commodity as far as I could see in those days. Then of course the '60s happened and the Beatles happened. I was working at WCLV in 1965 doing a classical music review, new releases, the Audition Booth.
>
> It mutated into the Perlich Project:
>
> I was doing folk music, humor, far out things like Sun Ra, Alan Ginsberg, bebop. I didn't know what I was doing. I was trying to be eclectic, and I don't know that there is a true category today. I would play Ravi Shankar, early Dylan, Glenn Gould, "Howl"—I went to the limit as far as I could, and it was very popular. I was interviewing Devo in the '70s, and they said, "We should interview you, we were listening in Akron." —**Martin Perlich, DJ, author**

One key link between AM and FM in Cleveland was Billy Bass, who worked at WIXY, WNCR, and finally, MMS. Wain raised his profile and then some.

Notable Cleveland Rock and Roll DJs of the 1960s

Wash Allen, WABQ
"Big Jack" Armstrong, WKYC, WIXY
Victor Boc, WMMS
Ron Britain, WHK
Jerry Brooke, WIXY
Chuck Dunaway, WKYC, WIXY
Bob Friend, WHK
Jerry G, KYW
Ken Hawkins, WJMO
Johnny Holliday, WHK
Dick "Wilde Childe" Kemp, WIXY
Lou "King" Kirby, WIXY
Jay Lawrence, KYW
Larry Morrow, WIXY
Bobby Magic, WIXY
Harry Martin and "Specs" Howard (Jerry Liebman), KYW, WKYC
"Emperor" Joe Mayer, WHK, WGAR, WWWE
Larry Morrow, CKLW, WIXY
Steve "Doc Nemo" Nemeth, WXEN, WZAK, WNCR
Martin Perlich, WCLV, WNCR
Bill Randle, WERE
Carl Reese, WHK
Mike Reineri, WIXY
Jim Runyon, KYW
Jim Stagg, KYW
Lynn Tolliver, WJMO
Big Wilson, KYW
Jerry "J.L." Wright, WJMO

Notable Cleveland Rock and Roll DJs of the 1970s

Ted Alexander, WBBG
Lee Andrews, WNCR, WMMS, WGCL
Billy Bass, WIXY, WNCR, WMMS
Tim Byrd, WGCL
Ed "Flash" Ferenc, WMMS
Ted Ferguson, WMMS
Joe Finan, WHK
Bill Freeman, WMMS
Len "Boom Boom" Goldberg, WMMS
Bob Gott, WGCL
Joyce Halasa, WMMS
"The Real" Bob James, WGAR
Doug Johnson, WWWM (M105)
Dick "Wilde Childe" Kemp, WMMS
Tom Kent, WIXY, WGCL
Jeff Kinzbach, WMMS
Lou "King" Kirby, WMMS
Betty Korvan, WMMS
John Lanigan, WGAR
Matt "the Cat" Lapczynski, WMMS
Joe Mayer, WGAR
Larry Morrow, WIXY
Tom Rezny ("T.R."), WWWM (M105)
Denny Sanders, WMMS
Murray Saul, (on-air personality) WMMS
David Spero, WMMS, WWWM (M105)
Bill Stallings, WWWM (M105)
Ginger Sutton (Steve Sinton), WNCR, WMMS
Lynn Tolliver, WGCL
Kid Leo (Lawrence Travagliante), WMMS
Bob Vernon, WGAR
Shauna Zurbrugg, WMMS

Norman Wain, the owner, said, "I don't know what people see in you, you're not a good jock, but for some reason people like you so we want to give you a shot at WIXY." Of course I wanted to do it, but could I do it? Could this no-talented, untrained person be in the same room with the greatest disc jockeys in the world, Chuck Dunaway, the Wilde Childe, Mike Reineri, Larry Morrow, Lou "King" Kirby, Chuck Knapp? I forgot the biggest guy: Jack Armstrong. I was scared to death, and Norman said, "Look, I'm going to put you on all night, midnight to six, but I'm going to give you your own show from 6 to 10 on Sunday nights to do whatever you want." WHK-FM changed call letters to WMMS in 1968. I said okay; I did the WIXY format on the weekdays overnight and learned how to be a Top 40 jock, but on Sunday I did Billy Bass and Friends. At WMMS, I thought I was popular. It was a drop in the bucket compared to the audience I had on Sunday night at WIXY 1260. If ten people heard me on WMMS, a thousand people heard me on WIXY. WIXY became a way of life. —**Billy Bass, DJ**

"If ten people heard me on WMMS, a thousand people heard me on WIXY. WIXY became a way of life."

The WIXY Allstars was a basketball team that played high school staff for charity, also played teachers. We never lost a game. Billy was there from '69 to around '72, and wherever I took the Larry Morrow Allstars we packed the place. Everybody wanted to see Billy Bass. When he was on NCR—this predates MMS—he was playing, like, the twenty-minute cut of Iron Butterfly's "In a Gadda da Vida," and nobody was doing that. When MMS started, Billy Bass was the reason MMS became so popular. I remember telling Walt

WIXY SUPERMEN: Billy Bass (in glasses) shares the bleachers with (from left) Chuck Knapp, Mike Reineri, and the pensive Larry Morrow.

Tiburski, who was my intern at WIXY, who then became the general manager of MMS, that Billy Bass ought to pull down his pants and have every one of the MMS disc jockeys kiss his butt for what he did for the station.
—Larry Morrow

In the late '60s and early '70s, free-form, or underground, radio was giving DJs the opportunity to personalize their programming by playing long, experimental album cuts. The era of Top 40 and the 45 rpm single was passing.

Bass and I used to get together on a regular basis for breakfast at the Forum Cafeteria on East 9th Street, just south of Euclid Avenue. Bass was doing his all Sunday night WIXY thing at the time, we'd go to breakfast at 7 in the morning. There was one morning where I'd just finished reading a long *Billboard* article on the FCC saying stations that simulcast their AM programming on their FM signal had to become more diverse and play separate programming on their FM station. So I said to Bass, why don't we start a radio station? I suggested to Bass that we go see Perlich. We pitched the idea to Martin and we came away from there agreeing that I would write up a programming proposal and present it to Nationwide [Nationwide Insurance, which then owned WGAR and WGAR-FM].

Nationwide hired some college students from CSU. It worked out so well that they called us again, and Bass suggested they hire Martin as a first step; they did, and that worked out so well, they came back and hired Bass. That was kind of like the first phase of the history of NCR-MMS, a continuum.
—Larry Bruner, former manager of La Cave

In 1970, the year *Scene* began publishing, Bass was riding high at WIXY. But he couldn't refuse the NCR offer.

The general manager offers me the program director's job at WNCR, like $500 a week. I was doing well at WIXY, but this was actual salary. So I took that job and hired Martin Perlich and David Spero and put the first woman on the radio in Cleveland as a disc jockey, Shana Zurbrugg. Now, the counterculture has grown. We got people working at banks who are antiwar. We got politicians who are antiwar, people on TV being antiwar.

So now we could take an antiwar stand on the radio twenty-four hours a day, and basically WNCR's purpose under my direction was to entertain the people with music, but most importantly it was to raise the consciousness about ending this horrible nightmare for all of these friends and relatives getting killed over in Vietnam. I'm not as smart as Martin Perlich; I wasn't feeling it from a geopolitical point. I was just feeling it from people I knew;

Cleveland's Rock Radio Stations of the 1950s–1980s

1950s

WDOK 1260 AM
WERE 1300 AM
WHK 1420 AM
WJMO 1490 AM
WJW 850 AM

1960s

CKLW 800 AM (Windsor, Ontario)
KYW/WKYC 1100 AM
WHK 1420 AM
WIXY 1260 AM
WJMO 1490 AM

1970s

CKLW 800 AM
WGAR 1220 AM
WGCL 98.5 FM
WIXY 1260 AM
WLYT 92.3 FM
WMMS 100.7 FM
WWWM (M105) 105.7 FM
WNCR 99.5 FM
WZZP 106.5 FM
WELW 107.9 FM

1980s

WCZR 107.3 FM
WDMT/WPHR 107.9 FM
WLTF 106.5 FM
WMJI (formerly M105) 105.5 FM
WMMS 100.7 FM
WNCX 98.5 FM
WONE 97.5 FM
WRQC 92.3 FM

my own half brother went to Vietnam and died there, and none of this was making any sense to me, so whatever I could do in my little, small way, that was what it was all about. —**Billy Bass**

By 1973, the classic MMS lineup was in place, with Bostonians Denny Sanders and John Gorman in charge as, respectively, program director and music director. They hired legendary DJs such as Kid Leo, Bass, Spero—and, over the years, Ed "Flash" Ferenc, Jeff Kinzbach, and Matt "the Cat."

At the beginning, MMS felt like a new community:

I was so a local kid, Euclid senior high and Cleveland State University. Got my degree in civil engineering. Our college radio station spawned Kid Leo, Matt the Cat, Betty Korvan [Bez Korovan], Ed "Flash" Ferenc, and myself, all came out of Cleveland State's closed-circuit radio station. It was awesome, and so two years in I discovered these guys, first time I smoked dope and six months before I graduated realized I wanted to make my life doing radio and my brother told me to finish school so I would be a marketable commodity. Three days after graduating with a civil engineering degree, I was working at the record store [Music Grotto, on East 24th Street], probably for about $1.75 an hour. —**Larry Bole, fan (Cleveland)**

THE UNITED UNDERGROUND FRONT:

The original WMMS staff was a powerhouse, indeed. Clockwise from top left: Joyce Halasa, Tom "Tree" Kelly, Shauna Zurbrugg, Martin Perlich, Billy Bass, Denny Sanders, David Spero.

This was a wonderful opportunity for all of us to really get in before FM was all that important—remember, this is 1973—and that was it. We got in before anybody paid attention to FM radio so we were able to create an image. The chemistry was fabulous. Everything worked. And for ten years there was barely an on-air lineup change. That never happens. —**Denny Sanders, former WMMS program director**

Denny and I had radio experience and a staff that hadn't had much radio experience, so we were able to sculpt the station to something that was unique. Right from the beginning, we said we wanted to be the biggest radio station in the country and we could see the possibilities. We were going to play music for its merit, we didn't care if it was old or new, it wasn't, as a lot of people feel, a free-form station. The staff had a lot of freedom to play what they wanted, but you had to play something from category A, B, and C, which forced everybody to play different kinds of music.

The one thing album rock stations did is they were programming strictly to a counterculture. You'd go to Coventry; it was a tiny counterculture but it was there nonetheless. But you could see this was a city ready to break out, and as we started playing acts like the Alex Harvey Band, Suzi Quatro, Roxy Music, we started getting this response from our audience. And we realized we were hitting upon something. We were not only reaching the counterculture, we were converting the culture, period. We were turning people on to a wider variety of music than since the days of Top 40, and Cleveland did have great Top 40 radio.
—**John Gorman, former WMMS music director**

THE UNDERGROUND GOES MAINSTREAM:

WMMS was the WIXY of the '80s when this photo was taken. Back row, left to right: John Gorman, Bill Freeman, Tom "T.R." Rezny, Ed "Flash" Ferenc, Jeff Kinzbach. Front row, left to right: Elizabeth Pick, Rhonda Kiefer, Matt "the Cat" Lapczynski, Denny Sanders, Betty Korvan, Len "Boom Boom" Goldberg, Kid Leo, Dia Stein, Tom O'Brien, Jim Marchyshyn.

"We were not only reaching the counterculture, we were converting the culture, period."

MMS was your touchstone. WMMS and *Scene* magazine for people of that age, and in terms of us, our growth pattern, they needed something positive or something they thought was positive, something to get above the bullshit they were living in. —**Michael Stanley, musician**

The Bird Is the Word

When I first moved here, I moved to East Cleveland. At night I'd hear gunfire. My drive to and from work was going down Euclid and the station was at 55th and Euclid, roughly. There used to be a sign at 55th and Euclid saying you're entering Mayor Perk's Model Cities program, and the sign was half-faded. As soon as you drove up to that railroad bridge where the sign was, it really was Desolation Row, it was like the Bronx, and you didn't really see any sign of life until East 105th and Euclid. Other than Severance and Case, it was a pit. It looked like a dying city. And the original WMMS had no windows. It was like a bunker. You'd get out at the end of the day, get in this parking lot where people were constantly having their cars stolen.

THE BIRD IS THE WORD:

First, it was magic mushrooms. But as 'MMS gained power, it took wing as the Buzzard.

One day Denny and I were talking about the WBZ logo [a famous symbol of Boston radio] and that night I'm driving home. It had to be January, February, a particularly lousy gray day and you're reading about these Fortune 500 companies moving out and how Mayor Perk raided the school funds, and what would you expect to see flying over the city but buzzards? And all of a sudden it makes sense. The next day, we talk and Denny likes the idea. The salespeople said, "You're trying to praise Cleveland's failures." I'm saying, "Exactly. Why not tell the truth about this frigging city?"—**John Gorman**

The Belkins, the Buzzards, and Budweiser were like a three-legged stool.

Everybody was pulling the rope at the same time. Everybody was working together; it was a client-based, band-based, record-based relationship. Everybody had an agenda, but everybody's agenda was one another's. So it was all tied in, so people like Kid Leo would say go see this band, people would go see it. —**Barry Gabel, promoter**

It was absolute synergy. This couldn't happen again. What put Cleveland on the map was, everything did line up right: the music scene, the musicians, retailing, lifestyle, radio stations—none of them could have made it on their own as successfully or for the length of time.

"What put Cleveland on the map was, everything did line up right: the music scene, the musicians, retailing, lifestyle, radio stations"

The Agora was perfect as an MMS outlet because of Hank's ability to get to the right bands and with the record people. Record companies were either trying to break new acts or records or get airplay, with Hank going to MMS to do live broadcasts and letting him be the key sponsor. Again, it was everything tied together, and the fans all wanted to be part of this. He put the fans closer to their music. You could always rely on them having good music, and there was this trust that the music MMS was going to play was going to be good, they were going to introduce you to the best of the best, the Agora was going to play it. When you walked into a Melody Lane or Music Grotto, it was "what's new this week?"—**"Daffy Dan" Gray, owner of Daffy Dan's**

There was that period of time during the '70s and part of the early '80s where the sports teams all sucked in town; the Indians were crap, the

Browns might have some seasons where they were sometimes OK, and the Cavs had some sort of the miracle of '76. Some of the guys at MMS were kind of superstars to people like me, like Kid Leo, Denny Sanders, Matt the Cat. We had a radio station that broke Bowie, and Springsteen always comes here, breaking acts like that; even during those years when they were winning all those contests in *Rolling Stone,* I never had any problem with their stuffing the ballot box because there weren't any rules that said you couldn't.

People could ride your ass for being from Cleveland, but you could always say we've got great radio; somebody would come out with a new album, they'd have the world exclusive. The station had given the city of Cleveland, for a number of people, some sense of pride and identity they could latch on to despite the river burning, the mayor's hair on fire, the city in default. For a while they gave the city something to feel good about. —**Chris Jacobs, fan (Rocky River)**

KID LEO

By 1975, Lawrence "Kid Leo" Travagliante had become as popular as the Buzzard itself and a celebrity in his own right. He could promote. He could create a star. He had the audience in the palm of his hand for years.

I came of age in the mid- to late '70s, when rock and roll in Cleveland reached its zenith. My girlfriends and I lived for Fridays at 6 P.M. when Murray Saul did the weekend countdown on MMS capped by his "you gotta, gotta, gotta, gotta, gotta get DOWN dammit!" routine, followed by the era's rock anthem, Springsteen's "Born to Run." With the radio blaring in my bedroom as I got dolled up for a night cruising up and down Lorain Avenue with the girls in my friend Maureen's Impala, it was thrilling and sexy and, for those days, kind of subversive.

WMMS was our touchstone—everything revolved around the oh-so-cool radio station and its rock-star-like DJ personalities. I was in love with the raspy-voiced, dark-haired Kid Leo, and remember a visit to the station as editor of my high school newspaper. He and Matt the Cat genially posed for photos and signed autographs for the geeky high school press; I was in heaven. To cap it off, they gave away albums by a new artist I had never heard of. I took the album home and was blown away by Meat Loaf's operatic, over-the-top *Bat Out of Hell.* Cleveland was one of his breakout markets. —**Patty Sheehan, fan (Strongsville)**

Murray Saul and his "Get down" made waves—for years.

Murray Saul would go on a rant, a rampaging rant. You could hear the spit flyin' off of him, and I remember him saying 'It's bee week, eat your honey.' He would put everything into it—he sounded like he was having a coronary every Friday at five o' clock, and then they'd play 'Born to Run.'"

Once, at a free concert in 1977 featuring Frank Marino and Mahogany Rush, I saw Saul standing off by himself.

Some Radio Station Call Letter Explanations

WGAR: George A. Richards (station owner)

WGCL: General Cinema

WHK: H. K. Carpenter, the station's first GM and VP

WIXY: Chosen by Mrs. Norman Wain because it sounds like the dial position "1260"

WJMO: For founder Wentworth J. Marshall; later, the station said it stood for We Jam More Often

WWWM: The "M" reflects the 51% ownership of Nick Mileti, with the Embrescia family owning 49% of that station; the station said it also stood for music

WMJI: Majic

WMMS: MetroMedia Stereo

WNCR: Nationwide Communications

WNCX: North Coast Express

WXEN: Xenophon Zapis (station owner)

(courtesy of www.cleve-radio.com)

BRANDING THE BUZZARD:

Jeff and Flash's Morning Zoo was a wakeup call for millions of northern Ohio-ans during the '80s. Cereal like this helped spread the word.

He was definitely an older guy in a crowd of young idiots who were partying and having a good time, so I walk over to him and I say, "Hey, Murray" . . . he was real cool. And my girlfriends walk over and it's like, what are you doing with this old guy? We're all like sixteen or seventeen. And I said, you guys, it's Murray Saul. They start screaming, and I go, "Do it." They want him to do a "Get down." He got angry and he said no. I didn't blame him at all; he would have been mobbed. He was sitting back with a joint and he did not want to bring attention to himself. That was it. It's a fond memory. My girlfriends respected the fact that he didn't want everybody to know who he was. —**Carole Singleton-Chase, fan (North Olmsted)**

What radio station did I listen to? WIXY 1260. The other station I used to like was KYW, now WTAM. They used to have a disc jockey named Jerry G, he kind of had not as deep a voice as Larry Morrow, not as resonant. He seemed to really relate to the kids kind of thing. To me, however, the all-time disc jockey in Cleveland was Johnny Holliday, WHK. I think it's because he was the top DJ in town when I first discovered music, which would have been early '62, '63, right before the Beatles. My sister was seven years older and I used to think the music she listened to was horrible—Elvis, that type of thing. The first people I liked were the Beach Boys, Beatles . . . *Meet the Beatles* was the first album I bought, at Zayre's.

"You usually associated early FM radio with free-form music. But to me it was as much about the personalities as it was the music."

Johnny Holliday was the fastest-talking DJ around. He was the guy who helped me discover music. WHK was fabulous. And then WIXY came in. After WIXY, there was FM. By the time I got back from college, there was MMS. You usually associated early FM radio with free-form music. But to me it was as much about the personalities as it was the music. But the way they blended, it was kind of a gestalt kind of thing. It had such a blue-collar kind of attitude to it; that was another element that made it what it was. I think people huddled around music, that's why that radio station was such a big deal at that time. —**Ed Watkins, fan (North Olmsted)**

Deflating the Buzzard

I'm the new rock critic at the *Plain Dealer* and Jeff and Flash ask me to come on to talk about the previous night's rock concerts on the Morning Zoo on MMS. I wanted to create an audience for myself and make people aware I was the new guy in town, and get a reading audience for myself. But after a while, it was tough to get up after a long night at a concert; they wanted me in probably between 8 and 9, they probably considered their [segment] prime drive time. So I start doing it and realize I don't really like these guys or what they're doing. After I did it for a couple of months, I thought, what am I getting out this? Nothing. So I called them and said I'm not going to do this anymore. They were like, how dare you? We bought you lunch. That only gave me more resolve. I'm like, I'm not on your payroll. So I just quit doing it and they started criticizing my reviews on the air. Jeff Kinzbach got on this thing where no rock bands will ever come here because Michael Heaton's mean to them. Then I would write a column making fun of Jeff Kinzbach for saying that about me.

A kid named Steve, who was the weekend engineer at MMS, lived in the same apartment building as me. One time he's over at my apartment watching the Steelers game and he said to me, "I saw a memo that came out that's in everybody's mailbox that seems to indicate that they stuff the ballot box on this *Rolling Stone* number one radio station in the country contest." My reporter antennae went up. "What do you mean by that?" He said, "There's a memo in everybody's mailbox, it just said everybody please come and help Joe and Sally; Sam's going to pick up the 10,000 *Rolling Stone*s and there's going to be pizza there." I said, "If I drove you down there right now, could you get me a copy of that?" He said yeah. I'm parked in my car with sunglasses on. He went in, made a copy of the memo, came back out, jumped in my car.

We sat on it a little bit because they were waiting to announce they had won the contest for the tenth year in a row. I went to the head of MMS at the time and said we're going to run a story tomorrow, etc. He says that's a lie, I deny it, if you print it, we'll sue you. Then I show him the memo and he reads it and he says everybody does it. I wrote it down. The day the story ran, Jeff and Flash spent four hours ripping me up and down, and Jeff started repeating his thing of no rock and roll would ever come here because of Michael Heaton. The thing that killed me—and I wish I had it on tape—he said, if I was you, meaning the wider audience of MMS listeners, the next time I saw Michael Heaton at a concert I'd go up and punch him right in the face. —**Michael Heaton, *Plain Dealer* columnist and reporter**

Notable Cleveland Rock and Roll DJs of the 1980s

Billy Bass, WMJI
Maria Farina, WMMS
Carol Ford, WDMT
Bill Freeman, WMMS
Len "Boom Boom" Goldberg, WMMS
Bob Gott, WGCL
Doug Johnson, M105
Brandy Kellogg (Catrina Severson), WGCL, WNCX
Betty Korvan, WMMS
John Lanigan, WMJI
Matt "the Cat" Lapczynski, WMMS
Jay Lawrence, WBBG
Bill Louis, WNCX
Tom Rezny ("T.R."), WWWM (M105)
Denny Sanders, WMMS, WNCX, WMJI
Bill Stallings, WWWM (M105)
Lynn Tolliver, WZAK
Kid Leo (Lawrence Travagliante), WMMS
"Dancin' Danny" Wright, WGCL, WGAR

MRS. BROWN, YOU'VE GOT A LOVELY DRUMSTICK: Herman's Hermits didn't stand a chance following the Who at Music Hall in 1967.

SHAKIN' ALL OVER

The British Invade Cleveland

A group so popular it drove kids wild, acts so hard-rocking they made the audience street-fighting men who couldn't get fooled again, and a group so psychedelic it created its own sense of time: The Beatles, the Rolling Stones, the Who, and Pink Floyd were among the biggest groups ever to hit Cleveland.

The Fab Four

The Beatles played Public Hall September 15, 1964, and Municipal Stadium August 14, 1966. Clevelanders had never seen anything like this.

The Beatles appeared on *The Ed Sullivan Show* February 9, 1964. Because it was my birthday, I got to pick the shows that Sunday night. There was this anticipation and something struck me there was something here I felt I could relate to. I wanted to be a part of this new music, whatever it was going to be called. And Monday, the group of us who were somewhat into music, it was like, did you see them? Weren't they neat? Weren't they something? And the buzz just got bigger and bigger. —**John Awarski, fan (Cleveland)**

It was more the rowdy crowd and the fact they had nurses on duty—who knew what was going to happen? All of the screaming made it seem more like an insurrection than a concert. You could not hear anything. At one point, I was thinking, who's that doing all that screaming? Then I realized I was one of them. —**Gail Ghetia Bellamy, fan (Cleveland Heights)**

Gail's husband-to-be, Steve Bellamy, was there, too, with his brother, John. He recalls scalpers offering tickets for $125, a fortune at that time:

My father was entertainment editor at the *Plain Dealer*, and when the Beatles were here, they stayed at the Cleveland Hotel on the square. After the Beatles left, the enterprising manager had the carpets taken up in the

ARRIVING IN HIGH STYLE:

The Beatles arrive in Cleveland at Hopkins Airport in September 1964.

BEATLES TAKE OVER THE WORLD, INCLUDING CLEVELAND:

Those lovable moptops drove the kids crazy when they made it to Cleveland in 1964. Thank Ed Sullivan for the introduction.

rooms and cut into four-square-inch pieces, two by two, and he gave them out. My father brought home one for each of his sons, and being young teenagers in 1964, we had no sense of historical perspective, so we looked at the carpet and said this is a dumb thing and we threw it away.

We were seated in temporary seating on the ground floor. When the Beatles came out, the girls started screaming so loud our ears rang for three days, and the only time the screaming abated somewhat—I mean it was like a continual note—was when they were about to start a new song, and by the time the crowd figured out what the song was, the screaming would go back up the scale, incredibly loud.

I think we were about three-quarters back on the ground floor, but we had a good view until people, primarily girls, started standing up on the seats, but the seats would kind of collapse on them, their ankles would get caught in the seat, they started screaming and panicking. So then they stood up on the arms of these portable chairs, it was like the Wave; the people who stood on arms in the front would have a ripple effect, and this made the chairs on these temporary pallets very unstable and they started going over like dominoes, and people would be trapped under a couple of those seats. No one was killed, but they did start taking people out limping, or who had fainted from the excitement.

Because the screaming was so loud, if you hadn't memorized the lyrics before you went to the concerts—everybody had because of the *Ed Sullivan Show*—you would not have known what they were singing. And also, elements in the crowd, primarily girls, kept rushing the stage, and someone came out to the microphone and said if you don't settle down or stop rushing the stage, the concert's going to end. They dropped the fire curtain, I recall, eight times, and waited until the crowd got under control before they continued on. We knew then that we were at one of the most important music events that we would ever be in our lives. —**Steve Bellamy, fan (Cleveland Heights)**

"They dropped the fire curtain, I recall, eight times, and waited until the crowd got under control before they continued on."

"People in the first maybe eight to ten rows were fine," recalls Clevelander George Shuba, who was snapping pictures in the orchestra pit for radio station WHK. "People in the eleventh row stood up so the people behind them couldn't see. By the time you got to the last rows, they stood on the chairs, and they collapsed because they were folding chairs. It wasn't a long show. At that point, I didn't even look down at my watch. My main thing was to get my photos and to try to document the stuff. And I was too busy battling the police and battling the crowds." A cop told Shuba to stop taking photos. A cop also told George Harrison to "cool it or I'm going to pull the plug on your amps." Harrison looked like he was going to kick the cop. "It settled down, the kids went back in their seats, and the rest of the concert went on. How long it lasted I couldn't tell you."

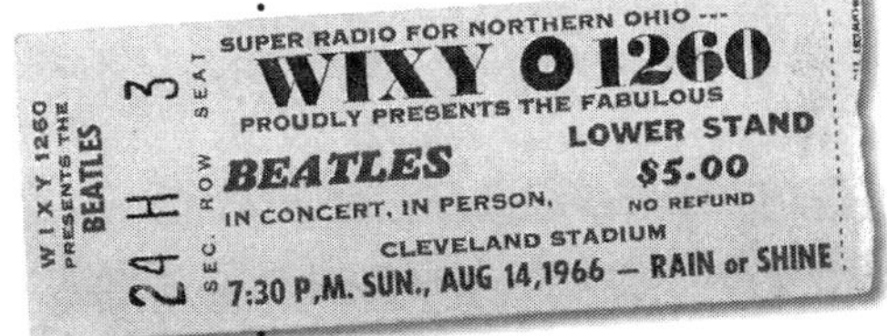

SUCH A DEAL:

The second and last time the Beatles came through Cleveland, WIXY made sure to keep ticket prices reasonable. The stadium wasn't even half full, though.

Promoter Eric Stevens, whose dad, Perry, was in the business, saw the Beatles both times and says the only comparison was with Elvis Presley:

At the Beatles concert in '64, it was a completely natural, unfettered explosion of human emotion. When they came out, Public Hall literally lit up with flash bulbs as though it was daytime. People were screaming at the top of their lungs. The din was relentless, but for some reason, John Lennon walked up to the microphone and there was a little bit of a lull; all of a sudden, you heard John Lennon sing "If I Fell in Love with You." I just get goose bumps thinking about it all these years later, and it's not nostalgia. So the kids started rushing the stage. Cops were not prepared for this at the time and they stopped the show; they threatened everybody, said we'll let 'em go on but you've got to stay in your seats, I think the house lights came on and the Beatles finished the show. I didn't come off the ceiling for at least two weeks. I was sixteen years old, a music freak and a radio freak—maybe just a freak. —**Eric Stevens, fan (Russell Township)**

The crowd was bigger at the stadium for the Beatles' second and last Cleveland appearance but not as big as it could have been.

A month before they came in, the Cleveland Diocese told people to stay away because Lennon said they were more popular than Christ and sales started dropping; we sold 25,000 tickets, we had the stage on second base, and the audience was basically between first base and third base, and in those days the police weren't trained on how to handle crowds so a lot of the policemen were watching the show when a teenage girl ran onto the stage; then a whole group of people started running to the stage, and my partners and I were in the position of tackling teenage girls. We had two limos parked behind the stage, one went for the first exit, the other to the second exit, and the Beatles were in the second limo. They themselves couldn't believe what was going on, they were overwhelmed with the kind of adulation they were getting. They were very innocent. Paul [McCartney] came to me and said, "I believe I could have any one of those women I chose." It was wild.

—Norman Wain, former WIXY executive

Beatles' Cleveland '66 set list, according to Sue Vendetti:

Rock & Roll Music
She's a Woman
If I Needed Someone
Day Tripper
I Feel Fine
Yesterday
I Wanna Be Your Man
Nowhere Man
Paperback Writer
Long Tall Sally

"I believe I could have any one of those women I chose."

There was a strange vibe because it was in the midst of the "we're bigger than Jesus" controversy. The Cleveland show was right in the eye of that storm. I know there were plenty of tickets available. We paid $5.50 for our seats. We were on the lower deck—you could hear 'em. The house system was the same speakers that they used for the Browns games. There was a weird electricity, especially when this kid ran out onto the field. That was like the first or second song. All of a sudden, we were closer, which was cool. I know it was during "Day Tripper," a lot of people had left their seats, the security consisted of snow fences and some cops, but there weren't that many for the crowd anyway. During "Day Tripper," a few people started breaching the snow fence and my brother goes, come on, we pushed right over it and suddenly we were on the field. I hit a trip wire in the field, went down, and ripped a pair of really nice, Sunday go-to-Mass pants. They were maroon and my mom was pissed. We got all the way to the stage. I touched the trailer the Beatles were in.

And then the WIXY 1260 DJs came out, said the Beatles are not coming back on, everybody cleared off, they pushed everybody back. Once everybody was cleared, they came back on and played their first song, "Rock and Roll

Music," again. If you put the two parts together, it came to about thirty-five minutes of total music. It was pretty cool. —**Bob Burford, fan (Kent)**

I remember the girl I went with, we were sitting in section 21, box 918, seat 22, and getting the tickets was a big deal because we went downtown real early in the morning; the stadium was the only place they were selling them as far as I know. My girlfriend's mother was the coolest thing. She took my girlfriend and two of her friends to spend the night outside the stadium to get tickets.

The concert was at 7:30. We arrived downtown at 4:45 P.M., went to the Sheraton Hotel, tried to get in but to no avail, went to the outside of the Sheraton and looked for the Beatles on the fifth floor, went across the street and looked for them again. We were told they were staying on the fourth floor. I called my friend who was at home and she told me my other two girlfriends, Donna and Debbie, were in the same hallway with the Beatles, with John and George—somehow they had gotten in, they just saw them. We looked for Donna and Debbie; they told us all about it. We went to the stadium, there was a limo that we rushed because we thought the Beatles were in there. Nothing was going on there, so we came back. We then looked for them, didn't see them. We rushed a fake decoy car. Too bad it wasn't them. Yes, too sad.

Talked to Donna and Debbie one more time. Show started at 7:55. Beatles came on after the Ronettes. The show order was the Remains, Bobby Hebb, Cyrkle, Ronettes, and the Beatles. Rushed the stage while they were singing "Day Tripper," stopped the show for about twenty minutes; the Beatles didn't want to go off stage, so they stayed on as long as they could. They were just getting overwhelmed—they went into this trailer, which in retrospect wasn't a very safe place to put the Beatles. They did come back on, they did finish the show. —**Sue Vendetti, fan (Brunswick)**

I was just so lucky; it was mezzanine, second tier, right in front of the stage, second row, and I got a pair of World War II binoculars, I could see really well. So the Remains come on, and what they had for a sound system at the stadium, there's this big delay, so the sound was pretty crappy. Bobby Hebb was also on the show, he came after the Remains, the "Sunny" guy; then the Ronettes came on; after the Ronettes came the Cyrkle. And all the while the sound's getting a little better. By the time the Beatles came out the sound was perfect. All I had to compare it to was my plastic Sears Silvertone record player.

I could see them sweat, they were fantastic, and McCartney was fabulous.

Some Groundbreaking Shows in Cleveland

Elvis Presley, Feb. 26, 1955, Circle Theater

Beatles, Sep. 15, 1964, Public Hall

Rolling Stones, Nov. 3, 1964, Public Hall

The Four Freshmen and the Christy Minstrels, Feb. 5, 1966, Music Hall (Jules and Mike Belkin present their first show)

Beatles, Aug. 14, 1966, Municipal Stadium

Terry Knight and the Pack, Sep. 27, 1966, La Cave

David Bowie, Sep. 22, 1972, Music Hall (first U.S. appearance)

Bruce Springsteen, Feb. 1, 1974, Allen Theatre

Roxy Music, May 26, 1974, Allen Theatre (first Cleveland appearance)

First World Series of Rock show (featuring the Beach Boys, Joe Walsh with Barnstorm, Lynyrd Skynyrd, and REO Speedwagon), June 23, 1974, Municipal Stadium

Bruce Springsteen, Aug. 9, 1978, the Agora

Michael Stanley Band, Aug. 25, 26, 30, and 31, 1982, Blossom Music Center

When the Beatles came out, they opened with "Nowhere Man." Everybody's screaming. How the heck did they get their pitch to open a cappella for "Nowhere Man?" And they did. They just knocked me out. They were everything I hoped they were but suspected maybe they wouldn't be.

They were in the middle of the stadium, lucky me; I'm right in front of them, in the second row. That was just chance; we just bought a ticket and that's the ticket we got. You could buy tickets at Sears or May Co. in those days. That was the providence of God. —**Norm Isaac, fan (Cleveland)**

I would have liked to have been Paul in the Beatles—and been in *A Hard Day's Night*. —**Eric Carmen, musician**

The Stones, July 1, 1978, Municipal Stadium

The stadium was the biggest venue in the area; it's where the Stones drew 82,500 to a World Series of Rock show July 1, 1978. (Actually, the stadium record was established September 1, 1974, when Santana, the Band, and headliners Crosby, Stills, Nash, and Young drew 88,000 to a World Series of Rock show.)

NOW FOR A REALLY, REALLY BIG SHOW:

Crosby Stills Nash & Young drew 88,000 to a 1974 World Series of Rock date.

We had seats in the lower deck, at about the 20-yard line. At some point during Stevie Wonder's performance, I noticed a scuffle to my left. I looked through the binoculars and could see two police officers pulling some guy towards them. It looked like they were trying to bust someone and it resulted in a tug of war. Then came a hail of cans and trash being hurled at the police, who took off running with their arms covering their heads. Not very long after that, one, then another, then another cop in riot gear started rushing onto the field. Before long there were dozens, with their batons drawn, pushing the entire crowd back into a corner. They then just stood there in a line, displaying their batons and keeping the crowd at bay. The whole place was booing what was happening. It continued for a long time and then the police retreated. One had to wonder what Stevie Wonder was thinking.

Next we began the wait for the Stones. After about an hour or two, people started to call out for them. Then clapping, as if calling for an encore. Then another hour passed. The frustration and anxiety kept increasing. Another round of clapping. Before long it was completely dark. It was hard not to feel despair. The waiting was endless. Then a glimmer of hope: way off in the distance, several small lights in the sky seemed to be heading in our direction—helicopters. By the time they landed, the whole place knew they were there. The excitement kept building and building. It took a while to set up and check the sound. The wait only made it more exciting. When the lights went on, Mick was flying across the stage and the whole place exploded. The opening chords sounded great. I have yet to see a more exciting or dramatic moment than when they opened that show. —**Michael Pierson, fan, (Chicago)**

> **"One, then another, then another cop in riot gear started rushing onto the field."**

Hard Scene, Harder Drugs

I was the co-coordinator of the Free Clinic's concert crisis task force. We worked all the tents. We did the Mosquito Dam Jam, a mini rock festival [August 28, 1976, in a state park in Trumbull County, near Youngstown], and Blue Oyster Cult was the showcase and they just didn't show up, so a riot ensued. There were probably 25,000 people there. You had to pay to get in; we didn't have to pay because we were the Free Clinic.

It was scary; it was a hostile crowd. The drugs had changed. It had gone from psychedelics to downers. Reds were big at that time: Nembutal, Seconal. So this was a very antagonistic, hostile crowd and it ended up with a food riot. Trumbull County sheriffs had to clear the place. They brought in dogs and everything. It was very ugly, it was horrible. The whole day was like that. There was an interracial couple that had set up a station for themselves in the middle of the crowd; they had put a blanket down. It was an outdoor show. Within earshot of them was a group of guys who had been drinking heavily, as was most of the crowd. And they were throwing racial slurs at the guy; his girlfriend told us at the tent. So he got up to protect the honor of his girlfriend and they pelted him with bottles.

So he ended up coming into the Free Clinic station for first aid. When he left the Free Clinic station, he attacked all three of those guys with a razor blade and slit two of their throats. Free Clinic workers throughout the crowd were able to stop the bleeding and save both of their lives. The crowd turned on the black guy, and he found refuge in the Free Clinic station and we actually ended up backing an ambulance into the station and put him in there with nobody seeing him and then evacuated him. There was like a lynch mob around us, with rocks in their hands ready to kill this guy. I don't

TUES., JULY 11th
Akron Rubber Bowl
8:30 P.M.
RAIN OR SHINE
BRING YOUR
BLANKETS
THE ROLLING STONES
and special guest star: STEVIE WONDER
TICKETS GO ON SALE SAT., MAY 27th AT CLEVELAND STADIUM, GATE C
Also at the AKRON RUBBER BOWL — 9 A.M. TO 4 P.M. BOTH LOCATIONS
TICKETS 5.50 ADVANCE — 6.50 AT DOOR
BELKIN PRODUCTIONS

THE WAIT WAS WORTH IT: Despite the hassles and the heat, the Rolling Stones show at the Rubber Bowl rocked the crowd.

Rolling Stones at the Akron Rubber Bowl, July 11, 1972 Setlist

Brown Sugar
Bitch
Rocks Off
Gimme Shelter
Happy
Tumbling Dice
Love In Vain
Sweet Virginia
You Can't Always Get What You Want
All Down The Line
Midnight Rambler
[band introduction]
Bye Bye Johnny
Rip This Joint
Jumpin' Jack Flash
Street Fighting Man

know if they arrested him, I don't know if he got charged with anything. He shouldn't have. That was a wild moment.

"It was scary; it was a hostile crowd. The drugs had changed. It had gone from psychedelics to downers. Reds were big at that time: Nembutal, Seconal."

As the drug culture changed, the World Series of Rock changed, too. Radically. In the beginning, with Crosby, Stills, Nash, & Young and those quote unquote head bands, there were a bunch of stoners in the crowd and the crowd stayed relatively mellow. Basically, what we were dealing with were LSD talkdowns, people who were getting agoraphobic. But as the drug culture changed over to a downer orientation, they passed a rule and said you couldn't take any bottles into the Stadium. So all these guys on the way into the Stadium at eight o'clock in the morning are getting shaken down for their liquor; they'd simply stand there and drink it, chugalug a whole bottle of tequila or bourbon, so they came in drunk. Then they would compound that with depressant drugs like Quaalude, Seconal, and Nembutal and we had a lot of near-fatalities on our hands. Fortunately, no one ever died in the care of the Free Clinic. At this point, we're talking '74 to '79. —**Quinn Stilletto, former Free Clinic worker**

There probably wasn't as much pot being smoked; the atmosphere wasn't as loving or giving. It wasn't the camaraderie you experienced in the late '60s or early '70s. I remember being on the infield somewhere around second base and people were pretty packed in, and all of a sudden, there was this big opening, and laying on the ground was a guy and a girl. She was bad gone, almost unconscious. This guy was hovering over there, and he looked like he was trying to throw up. So he kind of rolled over next to her. So they were all passed out. Lying next to them was a plastic milk jug full of this red juice with floating cherries on top, stemmed maraschino cherries.

What the fuck was in that stuff? I have no idea. I said to somebody, "Wow, what is that they're drinking? What do you think's in that jug?" And the guy standing next to me, who was half baked, looked at me and said, "I don't know, but if it does that to them, I think I gotta try some." Everybody just kind of walked around them. If that had been in the late '60s, somebody would have called for a medic. Here we were in the '80s or late '70s, and everyone said, fuck it. Now I just want to see how fucked up I can get. There were people kicking them. —**Jan Kallay, fan (Mentor)**

One of the most talked-about Stones shows took place in Akron July 1, 1972.

The Stones came in on a private plane and we had three or four cars, two of them police cars, to pick them up at the Akron-Canton Airport. As we're driving back to the Akron Rubber Bowl we heard a police report that there was a riot at the Akron Rubber Bowl and they were sending in an armored vehicle to control the problem. One of the policemen saw someone smoking dope and goes into the middle of this crowd and tries to arrest him. So everybody around them got up and police were off to the side, they called in headquarters and headquarters gives this message, and the Stones were in the car, and we figured that date was going to be gone. They were concerned. [Not to worry; the show came off.] —**Mike Belkin, promoter**

HE PLAYS BY SENSE OF SMELL:
Keith Moon just loses it. The drum kit, that is.

Me, Jim Henke, and two other guys drive out to the Akron Rubber Bowl at 9 in the morning, blazingly hot day. Everybody was just smoking dope everywhere. Commander Cody comes out, does a show, yahoo, very party atmosphere; at that time, there was this great sense of togetherness, the revolution, we're against the man, all that sort of hippie rhetoric. So during Stevie Wonder, a guy who was selling joints gets grabbed by cops down on the infield. People he's selling to grab him by the other arm. The whole stadium's watching this; no one's watching Stevie Wonder, and Stevie is like looking around, he doesn't know what's happening. So everyone starts pelting the cops with whatever is handy, mostly bottles. And the cops retreat; they let go of the guy, the hippies pull the guy into their bosom and the cops disappear and the whole stadium goes yaaaa, like for twenty minutes. Somebody in the band has by this time told Stevie, and they're kind of starting again, somebody in the band's going wow, you motherfuckers, you're cool. About ten minutes later, in the middle of another Stevie Wonder song, every aisle is full of riot cops with masks and batons. We're all going to die, something bad is going to happen right now. This is like the intensity of those times, so everything just chilled. Then the riot cops went away and it pretty much went without incident; the Stones came out and did a great show. —**Michael Heaton, fan (Bay Village)**

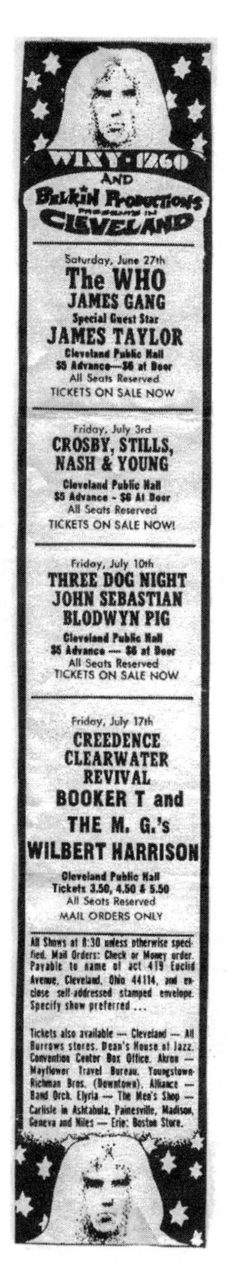

AND NOW FOR SOMETHING COMPLETELY DIFFERENT:

James Taylor seemed like a fish out of water opening for the Who at Public Hall.

TALKIN' ABOUT MY GENERATION

The Who is a favorite band of the Belkin brothers, Jules and Mike—and of many Cleveland fans.

We knew we were waiting for the drums to be kicked into the audience, for Townshend to smash the guitar, and we knew that Roger Daltrey would whip this thing around his head and sometimes kick it off his back foot into his hand. We knew that John Entwistle wasn't going to move because he was the anchor, and we knew that the smoke bombs were going to go off at the end and completely obliterate the whole arena. Keith Moon had some people dodging drumsticks and other people trying to catch them.

Here comes Peter Noone and poor Herman's Hermits, "Mrs. Brown You've Got a Lovely Daughter." The drumsticks that Keith Moon threw out started flying back at the Herman's Hermits drummer. A drumstick was tossed back toward the stage. I don't think it caught Peter Noone, but I think it clipped near the eye of the Hermits drummer. So Peter Noone stopped the show and bitched the audience out.

It seemed like there was a large contingent of the audience that had gone there to see the Who, though there were definitely Hermits fans there. At that point, Don and I said, we're outta here. We saw what we wanted to see.
—Jan Kallay, fan (Mentor), and Don Sebian, fan (Cleveland Heights)

"Peter Noone stopped the show and bitched the audience out."

I went to see the Who perform at Musicarnival in Warrensville Heights [on July 14, 1968]. I believe a band called Cyrus Erie was opening up for them, Eric Carmen and Wally Bryson were in that band; apparently the Who, who were quite famous for destroying their equipment, their equipment truck never arrived or something and they ended up using Cyrus Erie's equipment, or a majority of it. I don't remember them destroying it but I do remember Peter Townshend throwing a Shure Vocal Master up in the air and springing to the ground. And the Who were still wearing their fluffy Edwardian costumes. That was kind of comical; it was kind of a night filled with speculation.

It was great. I was sitting four or five rows from the Who. It was a theater in the round, a tent. They had the Who there, Vanilla Fudge performed there, all kinds of crazy bands performed there. **—Alan Greene, fan (Stow)**

Their PA blew up, I was able to get equipment to them, and they were able to go on. —**Wally Bryson, musician (the Mods, the Choir, the Raspberries)**

When I was at WTRX in Flint, Michigan, I was the first one to play "I Can't Explain," the Who's first hit. When they came to Cleveland, I was on WIXY. Belkin Productions sponsored the concert [June 27, 1970, Music Hall show with ticket prices $5 in advance, $6 at the door]. So first is the James Gang, a local group everyone loved, and then in the middle of the concert we were going to put this unknown guy who only had one record out by the name of James Taylor. And then the Who, the hottest rock and roll group in the country. The word was Belkin was really not sure whether this was going to work because we've got this heavy James Gang music, the Who, with 75 amps at that time; then you've got this little guy who walks out with a stool in the middle. He turns out to be a smash. This was at Public Hall, I think it was his debut. We went back to Billy Bass's house that night—Billy had a lot of people over after the concert—James Taylor came back to Billy's house in Cleveland Heights, I can still see James on Billy's steps going upstairs playing "Sweet Baby James" and all the songs that became hits.
—**Larry Morrow, radio personality**

ROGER DALTREY GIVES HIS ALL AT MUSIC HALL

The other weird concert also involved the Who, probably early '70s, or whenever the Who were on their *Tommy* tour. This time it was in the Music Hall. The Who did perform *Tommy*, but not until James Taylor opened by walking out to an empty stage with chair and acoustic guitar in hand, sat down, and played an entire acoustic set. That match-up was typical of that era, but weird nonetheless. At one point, with the crowd getting antsy, James said, "I feel like I'm performing in the middle of a football game."—**Bob Keesecker, fan (Willoughby)**

BIG SHOW, INTIMATE SETTING:

It wouldn't be long before Pink Floyd went huge, on the *Dark Side* and *Animals* tours. But in late 1971, the band played a gym. Those were the days . . .

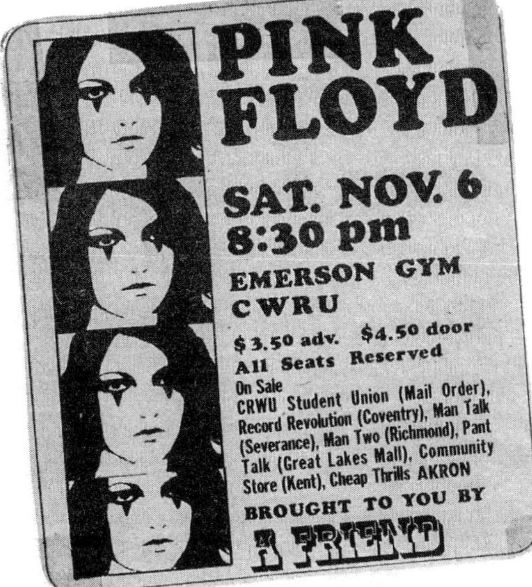

PINK FLOYD
SAT. NOV. 6
8:30 pm
EMERSON GYM
CWRU
$3.50 adv. $4.50 door
All Seats Reserved
On Sale
CRWU Student Union (Mail Order), Record Revolution (Coventry), Man Talk (Severance), Man Two (Richmond), Pant Talk (Great Lakes Mall), Community Store (Kent), Cheap Thrills AKRON
BROUGHT TO YOU BY
A FRIEND

One time in Cleveland, after the Who had finished a date, we were all meeting down at Captain Frank's for dinner, and it was a great show, sold out at Public Hall, and the whole band was there and a couple of guys from the James Gang and we don't know where Keith Moon's at. We look over to see Dale Peters, the bass player from the James Gang, walk in with Keith Moon. When he was playing that night, he was wearing all white. When he walked into the restaurant, he was wearing all wet black. He was inebriated and fell off the pier, which happened to be about ten feet to the water. Dale threw him a life preserver and pulled him out. It was the

Cuyahoga, it was filthy. If Dale hadn't been walking by, Keith would have never come around. Keith was happy, having fun, couldn't have cared less, he was soaking wet, sat down as if nothing had ever happened. —**Mike Belkin, promoter**

It was after a concert in Cleveland at the Coliseum, I believe, and we came back to town and stayed at Swingos for a party. This was when Keith Moon was into his police paraphernalia thing. Cleveland police gave him a uniform complete with all the accoutrements except for a gun. He had the badge, he had the belt, he had the nightstick, he had a pair of cuffs. Jane Scott was walking by. She said, "Leo, you know Keith Moon." He looks at me, doesn't say a word, sidles up to this blonde who happened to be standing in the area, takes out the cuffs, slaps one on her, slaps one on me. He walks away. This was a very good-looking woman, by the way. She totally just loses it. She is having close to a nervous breakdown: You don't know him, you don't know him, he'll keep us like this together. I drag her across the room, I went to him, said, "Keith, excuse me, she's having a hard time with the situation. Could you please take her cuffs off?" He looks at her, he looks at me, he uncuffs us, he says, "You're no fun," and walks away. The only three words he ever said to me. —**Lawrence "Kid Leo" Travagliante, former WMMS DJ**

BIG SHOWS, SMALL PRICES:

It seems like the Rolling Stones were one of the few groups to command double-digit ticket prices in the late '60s and '70s. Otherwise, the shows were a bargain, even for that time. That June 1973 ticket stub is for Pink Floyd's "Dark Side" show at Blossom. The Jan. 18, 1974 show is for Iggy and the Stooges—with Slade opening.

INTERSTELLAR OVERDRIVE

Frank Dutton helped with Pink Floyd's Allen Theatre show April 24, 1972. Tickets were $4.50 in advance, $5 at the door. It was an A Friend Productions show, courtesy of early Belkin competitor Roger Abrahamson. Floyd was touring behind *Meddle*, the show was a sellout—and dramatic.

They had an explosion at one part; I mixed powder for it. There was a big blast, there was a burn mark on the stage. It just kind of freaked everybody out for a minute. —**Frank Dutton, fan (Scranton, Pa.)**

The following year, Floyd was soaring behind *Dark Side of the Moon* and played Blossom.

Dark Side has become the anthem of the summer. MMS played it in its entirety around the clock. I and eight to twelve friends from Bay High School hear on the radio Pink Floyd is sold out, don't come out to Blossom, you can't get in. So of course that just means we all have to go. So we drove somewhere in a big van with all of us, guys and girls, parked five miles away and started walking through the woods to go and jump the fence. Suddenly we're twenty, then thirty-seven, there's like a hundred of us marching through the woods, long-haired hippies in flannel shirts and bell-bottom jeans, passing joints.

"There's like a hundred of us marching through the woods, long-haired hippies in flannel shirts and bell-bottom jeans, passing joints."

We get to the fence; it's been obvious that security is aware that this is happening. There's close to one hundred of us; there are like three guys standing there with the little Blossom security T-shirts on. The thing is just to get by them and run into the crowd. Suddenly we come in, we're like the army in *Braveheart* coming over the hill, they just turned and left. So all of us laid the fence down and went in. I think Blossom holds 18,000 and there were probably 40,000 people that night. We were the pig in the python, we had the weight, we were the deciders of what was about to happen. It was June 24, 1973. They played the album from beginning to end, and I remember standing at the top of the hill and feeling at one with the universe, and I walked down the hill all the way past these security guards and I was convinced I was invisible. —**Michael Heaton, fan (Bay Village)**

The scale was much bigger when Floyd delivered its *Animals* show June 25, 1977, as part of Cleveland's legendary World Series of Rock:

I think there were 81,000 people inside. There was a riot of about 2,000 outside, where they were breaking the windows and trying to get in. Everybody had blue jeans on, and the concert didn't start until 6 in the evening. We got there around eleven, twelve o'clock, the gates weren't open, they had those corrugated steel roll-down things over the gates, and these big, burly bikers beating the hell out of the corrugated things. They let us in hours early. You could bring coolers in, food. There'd be Frisbee playing on the field. If you were hungry, people would share.

It started out that you heard a plane coming and you look overhead, and this plane dives down into the stadium and looks as if it's going to crash into the stadium, and all of a sudden, it just goes up, and all of a sudden the band started and they were onstage, and that was the opening. It freaked everybody out, because the whole thing rumbled, you know? And the lights were on. It was fabulous. The thing about general admission then is you could go back into the stands and chill out or you could work your way up to the stage. I remember leaving around 11 because we had to catch the Rapid, the last train. They were doing an encore of "Money."

It was wonderful. I was never scared. Everybody was very loving. I remember the Free Clinic would have tents in case anybody did too much or whatever; the only thing that got out of hand was when they did this song "Pigs" or "Animals," they had these huge inflated animals coming down over a wire across the field, and some people got hold of the cables and tried to yank the cables, and Floyd said let go of the cables.

I think the last World Series I went to was the Cars and Fleetwood Mac, Bob Welch, I don't remember who else was there, but somebody did a nose-dive off the upper deck there. I remember seeing this guy come down; I don't recall what happened to him, if he was too stoned or he was just being an asshole. —**Tami Nato, fan (Parma)**

Oh, Pink Floyd, they did "Animals," they had the real airplane jets in the stadium, you're sitting there waiting for the show to start and all of a sudden you hear this roar and you looked up and this plane seemed like it just skimmed the top of the stadium and all of a sudden the music was on and they were playing. There was a lot of smoke in the air. —**Marie Vivolo, fan (Cleveland)**

Those were Quaalude days. Everybody's waiting and waiting and waiting for the concert to start and the Pink Floyd plane came up and flew down, sort of into the stadium. The stage was set on the east end of the stadium toward Burke Lakefront and it's cut out lower than the west side of the stadium. The plane actually flies into the stadium from east to west. The pilot or Pink Floyd got cited. You can't fly a plane into a stadium with 100,000 people; I think there was pretty close to 100,000 people at that concert. They were doing really cool things—like singing "Sheep," they would shoot these fireworks, they'd go poof, and little sheep parachutes would come down. Then they blew up their big pig, he was on a cable going from the center of the stage behind them, it went over our heads, it traveled up the cable to the top end of the stadium, and then it's coming back and the cable gets stuck and the pig starts deflating. We're hysterical, laughing. They come on this loudspeaker and say, please let go of the pig's cable. We're not going to play anymore until you let go of the pig. I think somewhere somebody got hold of it and the pig just stopped. They did let go and the music continued. —**Carole Singleton-Chase, fan (North Olmsted)**

PASSING THROUGH, PLUGGING IN

National Acts

Cleveland earned a reputation for breaking rock bands and artists. David Bowie went nationwide on the strength of his initial Cleveland shows, and Bruce Springsteen became the Boss on the basis of constant Ohio dates in the 1970s. Elvis Presley played his first concerts north of the Mason-Dixon Line here in 1955, when WERE-AM DJs Bill Randle and Tommy Edwards presented the Hillbilly Cat at the Circle Theater and Brooklyn High School. Many others made their mark here, too.

Belkin Productions promoted a lot of shows at a lot of venues. One that Jules Belkin found memorable was at the Akron Rubber Bowl on July 21, 1972:

> In those days, the cops didn't like the hippies, the hippies didn't like the cops. Of course we had to have cops there, it was part of the arrangement with the university [of Akron]. So there was always the smell of teargas.
>
> But when we did the Osmond Brothers we figured, here's a show that's going to be incident free. The audience was probably going to be nine, ten, twelve. It turned out to be a very warm night, so kids were standing in the infield, kind of crunched up against a barrier we would create in front of the stage. A couple of kids started passing out, so our first-aid station was underneath the stands in very close proximity to the Osmonds' dressing room. These little girls would be carried into the first-aid area and given water and as they walked out, they noticed they were right next to the Osmond Brothers' dressing room, even though the guys were out on the stage. The word got around if you went to first aid, you could be close to the Osmonds' dressing room. It was incredible. Kids were passed out all over the field. There were more down than up. Finally, we understood what the problem was.
>
> **—Jules Belkin, promoter**

Musician David Budin had some firsthand encounters with national talents at La Cave in the 1960s:

ON HER WAY UP:

It wouldn't be long before Linda Ronstadt went on her own. As a Stone Poney, Ronstadt played La Cave in 1967.

I was booked to play La Cave Memorial Day weekend 1967. They said I would be opening for some guy named Jim Hendricks, whom I assumed was the one who had been in the folk groups the Big Three [with future Mamas and Papas singer Cass Elliot and "Hey Joe" songwriter Tim Rose] and the Mugwumps [with Elliot, future Lovin' Spoonful guitarist Zal Yanovsky, and future M&P singer Denny Doherty], and who himself wrote the Johnny Rivers hit "Summer Rain" shortly thereafter.

But a couple of weeks before the gig, they told me that I would now be opening for the Stone Poneys (with future solo artist Linda Ronstadt, just as "Different Drum" was taking off), because this Hendricks guy, whose last name turned out to be spelled Hendrix, and whose first name was actually Jimi, had decided to play some festival in California in mid-June—the Monterey Pop Festival, which, of course, put him and many others on the musical map. But I had a good time playing with the Stone Poneys for five nights. And, in fact, I kind of kept in touch with one of them for a few years—except it was the wrong one; it was Bob Kimmel, not Linda Ronstadt. I mean, he was a very nice guy and a good musician and everything, but . . .

Then, a little more than a year later, in the summer of 1968, I found myself jamming onstage with Jimi Hendrix (not Jim Hendricks) at a club called the Scene in New York. But that's another story. —**David Budin, musician**

The Blues Project played La Cave a lot. So did its successor, Blood, Sweat & Tears, both the Al Kooper and David Clayton Thomas versions.

I had gone to New York City to visit my brother, who was attending Columbia University, for Thanksgiving weekend, 1964. He had heard Danny Kalb, who we knew as a folk guitarist, on the radio, saying that his new group, the Blues Project, was playing at the Café A Go Go that night and being recorded for a live LP. I knew Kalb had been on an Elektra Records compilation of acoustic blues artists called *The Blues Project,* so I assumed this was going to be an acoustic group of some kind.

When I got to the club, I saw electric guitars, bass guitar, organ, and drums set up and was initially annoyed, but from the first note they played, I was completely blown away. I went down to La Cave, where I told the manager, Stan Kain, about them and told him who their manager was, etc., and insisted he try to book them. At some point, Stan told me he had finally booked them, and they played La Cave the following June. Their appearance

BLUES PROJECTION:

The Blues Project made their mark at La Cave, Cleveland's hip-pest folk-rock nightspot of the '60s. Though the New York band was a spent force by 1967, it spawned several groups, including Blood, Sweat & Tears and Seatrain.

there opened the doors for more and more rock and blues artists at the club, which probably, ultimately, caused the club's demise. —**David Budin**

The Blues Project was huge at La Cave, but local acts did well, too, headlining clubs and opening for national bands. Richie Green reminisces about Bocky and the Visions, before he formed Richie and the Fortunes:

> We opened for the Rolling Stones first time they were here in town, 1964, Music Hall. [It was November 3.] I'm a kid just out of high school opening for the Rolling Stones. It kind of came pretty quick. We didn't meet the Rolling Stones, they weren't real friendly. They had a separate dressing room and didn't want to fraternize, which was kind of disappointing. We were their throwaway warm-up band, which was great for us. But there were other people who we opened for who were just super to us, like the Young Rascals, Lonnie Mack. This was the beginning of the British Invasion. The most notable thing I remember about that concert is that people were throwing soap and deodorant at the Rolling Stones. I guess they had some strange reputation. It was packed. They were immediately popular. —**Richard Green, musician**

Also there that night: Buddy Maver, then the drummer for Richie and the Fortunes, who would form Rainbow Canyon, Charade, and Charades:

> It was incredible. Here I was eighteen years old and we were all just young kids. Now they only drew about 6,500 people, but still, we went from playing little clubs with a few hundred people. That was quite a rush.

MICK STEPS IT UP:

Mick Jagger struts his stuff at Music Hall in late 1964. Even though the date drew poorly, it also show-cased local talent.

We also opened for the Dave Clark Five at Public Hall and for the Animals at Cleveland Arena, and we did a big show at Public Hall with Chuck Berry, one of those shows where everybody plays for twenty minutes. It included the Dixie Cups, the Shangri-Las, Four Tops, and us, and we had the coveted spot right before Chuck Berry. It was a Danny Thomas leukemia benefit. Berry kept yelling "leukemia" to the audience, which shouted it back; KYW was cosponsor. Berry wouldn't get off. This would be summer of '64, and Berry's pit band was old men from the Cleveland Orchestra. —**Buddy Maver, musician**

Here's a weird story about Tim Buckley, who died of an overdose in 1975. His son, Jeff, drowned in 1997.

Tim Buckley came to Cleveland and after his show [Buckley played La Cave in 1966] somebody brought him to my parents' house on Kenilworth Road in Cleveland. Tim Buckley appeared at the back door, and I think it was with Dave Budin, but he's not sure. We were all rather euphoric at that period, just in general. Buckley was with a girlfriend who had a hyper little poodle on a long leash and somehow my two brothers ended up taking Tim Buckley, who wanted to go swimming and was very high, to a pool at the Waldorf Towers on Overlook Road. So they sneaked over in the dark and crawled over the wall surrounding the swimming pool at the Waldorf Towers, that overlook Little Italy, and went swimming. Tim Buckley got really boisterous, and it alerted the residents of the apartment building, who were presumably inside sleeping. Lights started popping on in the apartment building, they jumped out of the pool, clambered over the wall, and fled on foot. —**Steve Bellamy, fan (Cleveland Heights)**

"We were all rather euphoric at that period, just in general."

Big Talent, Small Places

The Byrds played in Painesville at the Lake Theater, I'm going to guess around '65. I recollect it being around the time that "Turn, Turn, Turn" came out. For me, the Byrds were a great band. They were combining so many different things. The Lake Theater was like a regular movie house. In the band at that time was McGuinn, the two Clark[e]s, Crosby, and Hillman. It was astonishing. They played most of the first record and a bunch of the second, and their stuff, along with the harmonies, was the electric twelve-string guitar work. The place wasn't packed. —**Don Sebian, fan (Cleveland Heights)**

I went and saw the Byrds in Painesville, they played the Lake Theater real early on; Gene Clark came and thought I had stolen one of his harmonicas—I got backstage because I knew some of the people running it. It could have been '65, '66, '67; then the Byrds went out to Ashtabula and played a gig there. I was like a sponge as far as playing a guitar; I'd go see anybody I could just to try and pick something up. I had relatively small hands so I had to come up with different chord formations on my own to transpose and do different things. You had to really practice and rehearse and figure out what the hell you're doing. Even a gifted person who has a great ear and perfect pitch, you still have to learn how to play your instrument. —**Wally Bryson, musician (the Mods, the Choir, the Raspberries)**

Jimmy Page hit Baldwin-Wallace with the Yardbirds during an early tour.

Smoke and Mirrors

I got to be thinking, could it be around '66? Jeff Beck was the lead guitarist. I had read in *Tiger Beat* magazine this guy Jimmy Page was the new bass player in the Yardbirds, so on that show I expected to see Jimmy Page playing bass. However, there was no Beck; when they took the stage, Page comes out with a Telecaster, and Chris Dreja, the rhythm guitar player, is playing bass. So it was the *Little Games* format: Keith Relf, lead singer and harmonica player; Chris Dreja, bass; Jim McCarty, drums; Page on guitar. It's in the cafeteria at Baldwin-Wallace, and the stage was these little one-foot assembly risers, like if you had a glee club concert. It was pretty full; it couldn't have been more than five bucks, otherwise I couldn't have afforded to go.

I'm going to get chips and a Pepsi, I notice to my right Jimmy Page standing in the doorway smoking a cigarette. I was about fifteen and still very shy. What struck me was he had the whitest skin I'd ever seen. He was like a china doll, he was that pale. And of course, though he was very clean-shaven, he had this green five o'clock shadow and very big mutton chops. He was wearing a navy pea coat and striped pants. I'm freezing and I'm saying, do I just continue to get my Pepsi and chips or do I try to talk to Jimmy Page? I decided I am going to talk to him, and I would say, "Excuse me, are you Jimmy Page?" He isn't even noticing me, I'm getting the nerve and I'm starting to move toward him, he finishes the cigarette and just walks away.

There are no seats, so I snag a place on the floor right in front of the risers. To my amazement, I'm sitting right in front of them. I'm close enough to see the sweat rolling down his muttonchops. They start out the show; this

is when I realize there's no Beck. The first impression is the sound wasn't all that good, because you couldn't hear the bass. It comes time for the solo, I look at Page not knowing what to expect. He, too, blows my mind with a fantastic guitar solo. Nobody knew Beck had quit.

Joe Walsh drew massive crowds in Cleveland with the James Gang before he started playing with the Eagles in 1976.

So Keith Relf, after the first song, makes the mistake of saying "How do we sound?" And the other people, not just me, say turn up the bass. He looks at Chris Dreja, who's turning beet-red; I look over at his amp and I see the amp is on but the cord isn't plugged in. He moves toward the amp and pretends to turn up the volume, but I see he isn't really turning up the volume. After the night's over, I'm putting together that he was faking because he didn't know the part. I was just bowled over by Jimmy Page. Page has a white Telecaster and he's wearing white satin pants, and he had the big, thick mod belt buckle turned to the side so it wouldn't scratch his guitar. I'm thinking that's a good idea; I had been sent home from high school for wearing my wide-wale corduroy trousers because they said it wasn't acceptable attire. From that day on, I resolved to wear my belt buckle on the side.

The Choir opened up and they were the best band I ever saw. I think they were the first local band I ever heard that had more than two-part harmony. It was impressive; musically, they were excellent and tight. Vocally, they were phenomenal. We perceived them as real rock and roll guys. Wally Bryson, Dave Smalley doing most of the singing, Jim Bonfanti and Danny Klawon used to switch off on drums, and Dave Burke on bass. They said they had a new single coming out, they'd changed their name to the Choir. This was the first time I heard "Cold Outside." —**Norm Isaac, fan (Cleveland)**

The year is 1969. Location, Musicarnival, a tent in the round in Warrensville Heights. The draw is Led Zeppelin featuring Jimmy Page. Opening act, the James Gang:

James Gang opened up for Zeppelin; before Dale Peters it was Tom Kriss on bass, Jimmy Fox, and Joe Walsh. Their closing number, and this is like a month after the first Zeppelin album comes out, they do a little medley of vignettes, kind of a musical collage of Zeppelin stuff where Joe Walsh is doing all the great licks off that album. It was quite impressive. Soundwise, the equipment was not real good; it was in that era before you had a great concert sound. You could barely hear Robert Plant because of the sound system. Musically, it was a small enough place where you got to hear music really well.

Here's another view of that same Musiccarnival show:

When they played Musicarnival, we had front-row seats. It seemed like a medium-sized venue, enclosed by a large tent.

The James Gang opened the show—Joe Walsh was wearing bright pants. They didn't move around a whole lot, but Joe showed what a great guitarist he was, performing from the first two albums—"Funk #49," "The Bomber," etc. When they played "Lost Woman," I wondered if former Jimmy Page could hear it.

During the break, I was looking to my left and could see some people coming in our direction. Suddenly it was Jimmy Page carrying his famous Les Paul, walking right by us to get to the stage. They got up and played I think pretty much their first album. Sounded great. Page's guitar solos were amazing. They played at least one Yardbirds song, "White Summer," and of course the violin bow was used during a song or two. At the time it seemed extremely cool to see them—and in retrospect, it was something to see them before they got really big.

My friend and I were waiting for our ride, standing in the parking lot, when we saw some cool-looking guys walking toward us. Then we realized, wow, it was the group. I pulled out my camera and took a picture of Page as he was walking by. I should have asked before taking it, but he didn't seem to mind. We watched them walk to a small house in the middle of the parking lot and go in. We stood outside one of the windows, hoping for a peek inside, but no such luck. Headed home in the car, we realized that we were missing the telecast of man first walking on the moon, on July 20, 1969. We also realized that Led Zeppelin were probably inside that little house watching it themselves. [It was the home of Herman Spero, head of *Upbeat*.]

A couple months later, Led Zeppelin announced they were coming back to Cleveland again, this time playing the huge Public Hall. Grand Funk opened for them and played a lot of songs from their album with "I'm Your Captain" on it. They also played their anti-drug song and tried to rally the crowd with it. It was October 24, 1969.

With "Whole Lotta Love" on the radio all the time, the crowd this time was huge. When the group came on, Robert Plant was running around, wearing a construction worker's hardhat with an American flag design on it. I remember they did songs from their first

Robert Plant and his Zeppelin

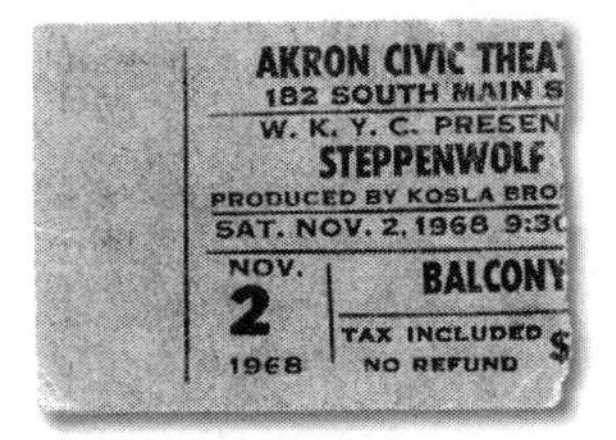

two albums. Our seats were, as I recall, about thirty or so rows back, on the main floor. Sounded great. —**Michael Pierson, fan (Chicago)**

The Race Factor

Racial tension occasionally contributed to the electricity of the time:

My brother decided we must go see James Brown in concert. So in March 1968, just a few months before Martin Luther King Jr. was assassinated, at the height of the civil rights movement, we lined up outside the Allen Theatre with tickets in hand to see the James Brown Revue. My brother was always one to only get "the best." Imagine my surprise when I found my skinny fifteen-year-old white ass in about the third row center waiting for the show to begin. As I looked around, I couldn't help but notice we were the only white people I could see! As we sat waiting for the show to begin, I must admit I felt somewhat uncomfortable.

"As I looked around, I couldn't help but notice we were the only white people I could see!"

In those days, although I was aware of and very sympathetic to the growing civil rights movement, I nevertheless had not spent much time with black people. I had grown up in Cleveland's Slavic Village, only seeing black people on the occasional visit to Euclid Beach, or maybe seeing some street people while shopping downtown with my mother. When we moved to Maple Heights in 1962, I attended public school for the first time and for the first time I met black kids. There were two in my fifth-grade class, and maybe a total of seven in the whole school. In Maple Heights back then, there really was an 'other side of the tracks' where the black folks lived. My sister raised a few eyebrows when she invited her black classmate from high school, Phyllis, to come walk home one night after school to do homework together.

So we're sitting there, front center, in the darkened Allen Theatre. James's opening acts had finished . . . and were enjoyable, when . . . all of a sudden . . . BOO-OM!! From behind drawn curtains, the James Brown Band crashes into a funk

ELECTRIC TEENAGELAND:

When Jimi Hendrix played two shows on March 26, 1968, fans lined the streets around Public Hall. These were Hendrix's only Cleveland performances.

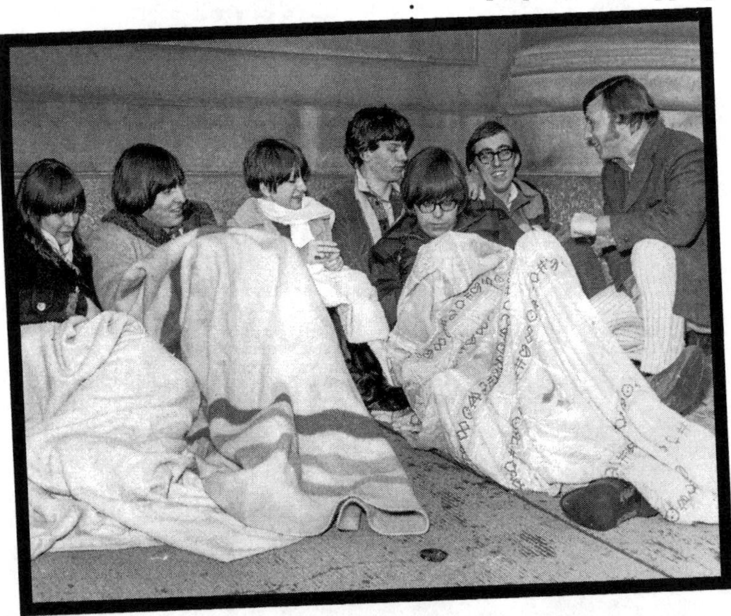

riff, full bore, full speed, with no intro, no downbeat, in full stride, as if a giant locomotive had appeared, in a split second, without warning, right in front of you, barreling full bore down on you. I about jumped a foot in the air, actually I did jump a foot in the air, and after my heart left my throat, the full beauty of this tight, super-disciplined, super-hot dynamite funky eighteen-piece band took over my body and every body in that hall.

From there, it was just amazing to see the actual James Brown, right there on stage, doing the splits, singing, growling, screaming, begging and pleading, sweating, throwing out cuff links to the audience and testifying. The audience never stopped screaming. It was just like a Beatles concert! I was a little uncomfortable when he took a bit of time out to allude to the unfairness of life under the man (white guilt) but I took it in stride and the music took over again. And I knew all the words, too. It was an amazing show! An incredible experience. —**Matt "the Cat" Lapczynski, former WMMS DJ**

TAKING US HIGHER:

Sly Stone at the Cleveland Arena.

My very first concert was December of 1973 at Cleveland Arena and it was Sly and the Family Stone. I was twelve years old. My mom took me. I loved Sly and the Family Stone, and she lived in an apartment building across the street at 49th and Euclid.; we just walked over there. It was a blizzard that night—they were coming from Detroit, they were driving, and they were late because the roads were so bad. It was snowing here also, so a lot of people didn't make it.

Once they got there, they said, "Come on down" and everybody like, rushed the stage. I was right in front. There were no bouncers; I could touch the fabric on his costume. Sly played organ and keyboards. It was wonderful. I do have snapshots of that . . . People were smoking pot, passing it back and forth. It was a lot of blacks, but it didn't bother me. I felt very comfortable . . . I had my little snapshot camera with the little flash cube that twirled around . . . Sometimes music, being the international language, brings a lot of love and harmony. —**Tami Nato, fan (Parma)**

After the Rolling Stones show at the Akron Rubber Bowl in 1972, Michael Heaton had this experience:

My friend Randy and I went back to the car and the car had broken down, Jim Henke and his friend had called one of their parents to come get 'em. We said fuck that, we're going to hitchhike home. So we did; whoever this guy was who picked us up thought it would be funny to drop us off on Hough Avenue in the middle of the night, the scariest, worst black neighborhood in Cleveland.

So we're walking through Hough, stoned out of our gourds. I had lost my shoes and my shirt, I was wearing some makeshift poncho out of a quilt and we're walking through Hough when some Cleveland cops stop and pick us up and say "What are you doing here? Get in the car." We were happy to and they drove us to the East 9th Street exit that goes to the West Side. And all the way over they're saying, "You know how lucky you are? You know those niggers would kill you for a nickel or a blowjob?" We're like, two seventeen-year-old suburban West Side white kids. Now it's about 4 in the morning and who stops to pick us up but some black guy, a cook or janitor going to work in the morning, and he gave us a ride all the way from downtown Cleveland into Lakewood. —**Michael Heaton, fan (Bay Village)**

Breaking Bowie and the Boss

By the time Sly played the Arena at 30th and Euclid, WMMS was hot—and pushing David Bowie.

One day the RCA guy comes in with a white-label disk in a white jacket, unmarked, says, "I want to play something for you, what do you think of this?" It knocked me out, it was fabulous. Who is that? Sounds familiar. It's David Bowie, we just signed him to RCA, the album's called *Hunky Dory*, his first album for us. So I played it for Billy Bass, who by this time was program director of WMMS. We got behind it as a radio station. The big cuts were "Changes" and "Life on Mars," and now it's time for Bowie to do his first tour of the United States and his first major performance was at Cleveland Music Hall. That was done primarily because of the success and buzz that WMMS generated for the record in Cleveland. I'm sure when they set the tour up they didn't want to do his first major appearance in Cleveland to half a house. We were pretty much given the credit for breaking David in the United States, and Bowie to this day recognizes that. —**Denny Sanders, former WMMS music director**

BOWIE MAKES HIS MARK: Cleveland had never seen anything like Bowie and his Spiders From Mars. The orange-haired space oddity and his spectacular band made their U.S. debut at Music Hall Sept. 22, 1972.

The reason I get credit for breaking David Bowie was I played the living shit out of the record and the record just took off here and the station used it because we were trying to separate ourselves from that Southern rock sound. We used the David Bowie album to do that.

The Belkins are the ones that brought Bowie to Cleveland. David Bowie, Lou Reed, and Mott the Hoople got big under my direction as director of national album promotion at RCA Records. David Bowie, Lou Reed and Mott the Hoople, as a DJ, I broke those records in Cleveland.

David Bowie was big in Cleveland because I was playing the record so much, but not anywhere else. Then it got big in Philadelphia, but it didn't get big all over the country until I started working for RCA and promoted the album all over the country. —**Billy Bass, DJ**

"I played the living shit out of the record and the record just took off."

In May 1972, Circus is playing out, the Raspberries' first album is making waves, records are selling for $3.50 to $6, Glass Harp is playing the Agora on East 24th for $2. Bruno-Whittington-Bruno is working at Otto Site on Columbus Road, and Tiny Alice is rocking the Viking Saloon, at 2005 Chester. Time for a jolt in the form of a guy with orange hair.

"Bowie's first American concert September 22, 1972, was a transformative experience for me. There was an electricity in the air about that show. We got tickets early; it was sold out. I'm not sure *Ziggy Stardust* was even out yet, but MMS was all over it, they were playing *Hunky Dory* to death almost. When we got there, every seat had a "Ziggy Stardust and the Spiders from Mars" bag on it, a little promotional bag. The bag contained a flyer for the Public Hall shows in November, they had already booked him to come back and he hadn't even played it yet. —**Bob Burford, fan (Kent)**

BRANDING BOWIE:
MMS, Belkin, and Bowie's record company were so bent on having a hit they papered Music Hall with flyers promoting a Public Hall show two months later. Both those Public Hall nights sold out, at 10,000 seats each.

At Music Hall, he sold 3,200 seats; when Bowie came back November 25 and 26, he sold out 10,000 seats each night.

When those lights went down and you heard the beginning of "Ode to Joy," this deep bass note, it was like you didn't know what was happening. There was a sense of what the hell's going on, Bowie walks out, looking like he's in a movie, with his orange hair and the Spiders from Mars in their full regalia. I certainly didn't know he was going to look like that; with *Hunky Dory* being my primary preference, I didn't realize, when Mick Ronson was doing solos, with one hand and he's doing "Width of a Circle," people were just going bullshit. Then suddenly Bowie would sit down and do a Jacques Brel song, "My Death." Bowie was a big part of the '70s for me; Bowie, Springsteen, whatever. Cleveland had been early on the record, and they thought Cleveland could make a greater impact than New York. It probably played out as well as could be expected. —**Bob Burford**

They came out like no other group I'd ever heard or seen before. It was just what they were wearing, the light show they had, and the guys in the group just looked so different than anybody else at the time. Plus the buildup: MMS kept pounding the concert at that time. —**Brad Bell, fan (Chagrin Falls)**

Two years later and it was time for a very different kind of star. Bruce Springsteen became the Boss over a single year: In 1974 and 1975, he played ten dates in northern Ohio. Eric Olsen saw him both years:

The first show was February 1, 1974. It was at the Allen Theatre. I and my best friend at the time, Bucky, went to the show; it was $5.50, and we were there to see Wishbone Ash. We were very excited about Wishbone Ash because it kind of fit all our criteria: they weren't household names, they were kind of discoveries, they were very cool in an English way.

Opening was this person named Bruce Springsteen, with the bizarre spelling of two *e*'s. Didn't give it a thought; never heard of him. Now this is a very classic '70s longhair, relatively stylish, reasonably well-dressed, classic Cleveland crowd, it couldn't have been more unlike what we were about to see in the opening act. Lots and lots of pastels, platform shoes. We were in the middle and maybe not more than twenty rows back.

Kent State Programming Board presents
BLACK OAK ARKANSAS
plus SPECIAL GUEST
BRUCE SPRINGSTEEN
Sat., Jan. 19, 8 P.M.
KSU BALLROOM
$4 ADV. $4.50 AT DOOR
Tickets available at all Cleveland Tux Shops, Mayflower Travel (Akron), Kent Community Store, Kent State Student Center.

This guy looks like a beatnik. He had short, curly hair, a beard. He's got this huge band, a bunch of people running around, two different keyboard players; he's very dramatic, hot where everything else about the place, the crowd and the band we were expecting to see, was cool. And he's very engaged with the crowd, talking a lot, doing all the stuff people don't do. The whole feel is like '50s R&B somehow brought into a contemporary setting with stories. There's this weird sort of urban/exurban feel—there's no suburbia. And the great majority of that crowd was suburban, I've always been suburban. And the music and the vibe is this weird combination of quite urban and rural.

So it felt very alien; I didn't know any of the songs, and the crowd because of all these things—plus it's an opening act—was very hesitant and just didn't really want to succumb to this entirely different worldview. It was rock and roll versus rock; we were there for rock. And this guy was rock and roll, very '50s-derived. But by the end of his not-long set he absolutely won over the crowd. Actually, it was sixty-five minutes; that's quite long for an opening act. No one wanted him to go.

I didn't see him again until August 8 of '75, at Akron Civic Theater. By then, Springsteen had been absolutely adopted by MMS to the point of deification, though it never felt like hype, it always felt earned. At that point still the DJs really did have a lot of say over what they played and each did have a musical personality of their own, so when they were really pushing something, you could tell they were pushing it because they really loved it. So it was Kid Leo pushing Springsteen, not in conjunction with some marketing campaign but because that's how much they loved him.

We were breaking a lot of the British acts, the proto-punks, the glammy bands: Bowie, Mott the Hoople, Roxy Music, that's what the town was known for. The bands coming out of here were very new wavy before the term existed, like Devo. So Springsteen, musically anyway, really didn't fit into it but yet he did because he was so genuine and so good. By then we knew the first two albums backwards and forwards; by mid-'75, he was really on fire here, Cleveland was Asbury Park West.

"By then, Springsteen had been absolutely adopted by MMS to the point of deification."

Bruce Springsteen shows the early form that made Cleveland "Asbury Park West."

On the way in they were handing out flyers at the door for a new Springsteen album to be coming out soon called *Tenth Avenue Freeze-Out*. That was the other thing leading up to this. "Born to Run," the single, had been out. So you had this near perfect album (*Wild and Innocent*) with these extended morality tales of "Rosalita" and "Kitty's Back" and "Incident on 57th Street" and then you had the blazing light of Spector summer with "Born to Run," that huge, booming production. "Born to Run" was a perfect summer single . . .

Where the first show laid the groundwork, this show with him as headliner, with everyone knowing who he was and wanting to be there, the single out, with those kinds of expectations and the literal electricity in the air, all of those expectations were smashed, transcended, crumpled up into little balls, ground into dirt, picked up and kicked down the street. It just kept going and going as he fed on the energy of the crowd and it continued to the point where the last three songs—a "Love So Fine" medley with "Having a Party" into "Carol" and winding up with "Quarter to Three"—there was nothing left. People were wrung dry. Every ounce of energy was gone from the band. It was the show where everything just was in place, went right, was perfect, was a steady build, with a huge peak in the middle—"Born To Run"—and then backed off into "Back Streets."

You had no choice but to participate. He worked the crowd so masterfully, you never for a moment thought you were being manipulated. You were feeding off each other. People were just literally ecstatic. People in the crowd became friends. You moved closer and closer down, so by the final of the encores, we were right near the front, just off the stage. It was incredibly hot; the doors were open, people were looking in on the show. When it was over, no one had anything left. —**Eric Olsen, fan (Aurora)**

One Springsteen concert even more embedded in Cleveland memory is his free show at the Agora August 9, 1978, in celebration of the tenth anniversary of WMMS. Emceed by Kid Leo, it drew 1,200 and is one of the most bootlegged Springsteen dates ever.

That show was just incredible. They gave away the tickets on a lottery basis. You had to send in a postcard to WMMS for your name to be picked, so some of my friends sent in dozens of postcards. I sent in a number of them, and sure enough, a good buddy got a ticket and I said, "Well, I'll go down with you and buy a ticket on the street." I thought $30 or $40 should get me a ticket. We're down there fairly early and there is not one person anywhere selling tickets. There was nothing but people looking for tickets, and I was starting to get worried.

I took a little bit of a walk away from 24th to some of the outlying parking lots and confronted people as they got out of their car. I looked for single guys. I got more and more brazen as I went. Finally, I went up to this guy and said, "Here's the deal: You just get right back in your car, I'm going to pay you fifty bucks, you're going to go home, you're giving me your ticket." One guy said yeah. It was outrageous that I paid $50, but this guy thought it was a pretty good deal. I didn't give him a whole lot of room to negotiate. So then I went in and that show was just . . . You can't make this stuff up.
—**Bob Burford**

This poster from the Agora for the week of Aug. 7, 1978 publicizes the Boss's legendary MMS concert that Wednesday, Aug. 9.

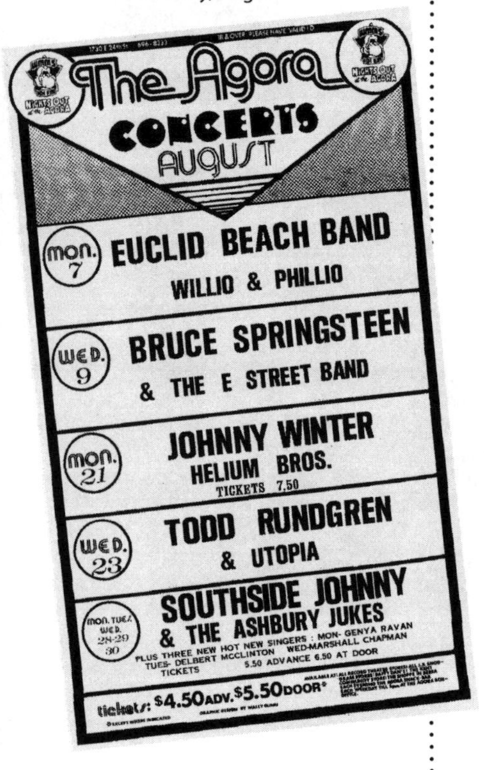

There was a period from '75 to the early '80s where I would see Springsteen all the time. Over four years, I saw him about twelve times. That show at the Agora was like a rock and roll high Mass at times. It was a religious experience, a revival meeting, a stadium show in a small club. There should have been 20,000 people there to see it. It was just an unbelievable night; but there were a lot of nights like that there. —**Chris Jacobs, fan (Rocky River)**

Certainly the tenth-anniversary concert with Bruce Springsteen at the Agora is hard to beat. Because of the power of bootlegs—this concert at the Agora was attended by more people than attended Woodstock, if you believe everybody—that's how legendary it became. Also, Bruce put me into two of his songs that night, "Growin' Up" and one of the encores, Eddie Floyd's "Knock on Wood." He made me a character in "Growin' Up" and referenced me in "Knock on Wood." That was pretty special, and it's because of the status that that concert has attained over the years that it's become more special. —**Lawrence "Kid Leo" Travagliante, former WMMS DJ**

"This concert at the Agora was attended by more people than attended Woodstock, if you believe everybody."

There's umpteen bootlegs of the Springsteen show from the Cleveland Agora. I've heard a handful of them, they're all pretty kind of rough sounding. MMS ran that live, and every year at Christmastime they'd run it in its entirety commercial free.

We had a copy of the concert at the station in the same format, and one Sunday Denny was on I said, you mind if I make a copy? I can honestly say I've pretty much kept it for myself. I admire a performer enough that that's their livelihood. They've worked hard to earn a dollar. I have it for myself and a handful of friends and that's it. To my knowledge, the sixteen-track masters from that night are over at the Western Reserve Historical Society as part of the LoConti collection [according to Hank LoConti, they're actually twenty-four-track master tapes]. —**Frank Foti, former WMMS engineer**

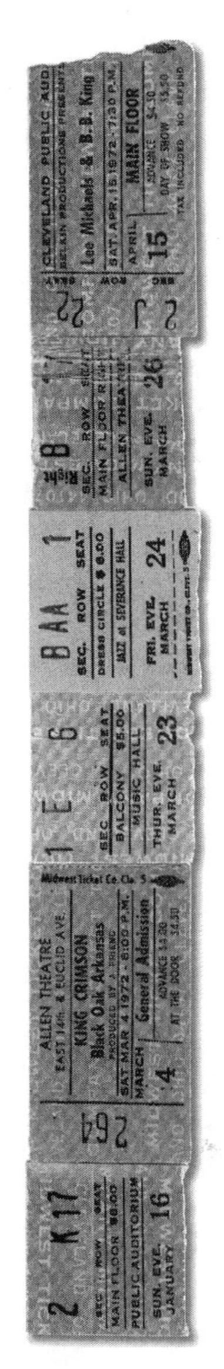

I ended up signing Michael Stanley, and I went to see him in Youngstown and the crowd response was so great, and at that time he hadn't done a live album. I think "Midwest Midnight" came out of a breakfast we had. I told him to write more about Cleveland, his thoughts on the city; Springsteen was going with Jersey, I wanted Michael to do that with Cleveland. This is 1974 or '75. —**Steve Popovich, promoter and producer**

I was the first one to write about him in Cleveland. I think I said something about him when he was at the Agora; he's my favorite. I don't want to say that, that's not nice. Say he's one of my favorites. His intensity, and it's just good music, it reaches you, and he has that little sense of humor, that little wink, he's nice to people. I said that he would be a superstar; the last time I saw him I gave him a copy of that.
—**Jane Scott, music critic**

GETTIN' JUICY: The Raspberries went from high school players to hit-making heartthrobs in just a few short years.

SO YOU WANNA BE A ROCK AND ROLL STAR

Local Legends

All bands start locally: Kids get together to make some noise. As word of the band spreads, the reach and the range expand. In the '50s, '60s, and '70s, Cleveland-area bands were primarily local, though some went nationwide, like the Michael Stanley Band, and even worldwide, like the James Gang and the Raspberries. Back in the day, you'd hear the Gang, the Mods, the Lost Souls, the Choir, and Damnation of Adam Blessing at teen fairs, in armories, at schools from grade to high, at clubs like the Mentor Hullabaloo and Cyrus Erie West, at colleges, at Musicarnival. AM radio, for sure, played them. FM did some. A few even got on TV.

In 1958, the Poni-Tails scored on the national charts, reaching number seven with "Born Too Late"; two years earlier, a similar girl group, the Tracey Twins, made national TV. Here's a look back at a night in 1956 on the *Arthur Godfrey and His Friends* show. "Tonight You Belong to Me," by Eudi and Euni Tracey, was a minor hit that year. Eudi Tracey remembers:

> We woke up to get ready to go to the airport to a huge, huge snowstorm that became the big snow of 1956. We couldn't get to the airport, so our father drove us to the train station. We had to be in New York by about 5:30 or 6 o'clock because the show went on at 8. So there we are with our bags full, because if you won the Godfrey show, you got a week's engagement on it, so we had to pack clothes—hopefully we'd be performing on this TV show every day for a week.

They arrived, exhausted, and the show threw them on first.

> How we sang was a mystery, but we won. The audience was cheering us, and when we won they applauded us and the strings did that thing with their bows. Arthur Godfrey himself wasn't there, he was away on vacation, so his second in command came up to us, said be on time tomorrow. That was charming.

TWILIGHTER TIME:
Steve Popovich was key to the Twilighters, the band he formed after Ronnie and the Savoys. This is one of their singles.

They sang "Give Me Love," a McGuire Sisters tune.

We were the very beginnings of rock and roll. We didn't know it, though. I loved everything. We used to do standards and movie music. We were at the Imperial Theater at 142nd and Kinsman all our growing up years; from the time we were six years old our parents would let us walk over. We were very annoyed that the USO wouldn't take us on when we were ten years old. **—Eudi Tracey, musician (the Tracey Twins)**

DOUBLE DYNAMITE:
Euni (left) and Eudi Tracey were cute as a button in their promotional photo. They scored a minor hit in 1958 and made it to the *Arthur Godfrey and Friends Show*.

"We were the very beginnings of rock and roll. We didn't know it, though."

The Roots of Cleveland Rock

The early '60s was a great time for bar bands like Steve Popovich's first group, Ronnie and the Savoys. Popovich had followed his mom to Cleveland from Nemacolin, Pennsylvania. Back home, Ronnie and the Savoys scored a radio hit with their Duane Eddy–style instrumental, "Slappin' Rods and Leaky Oil."

We were just thrilled to hear it on the radio, we'd play like two gigs on a Saturday night. Even the year I moved here, I'd come back on weekends. It was great money to make $12, $15 a night in high school in the '50s. We'd play three hours on a Friday night in Carmichael, a little town next to our town, tear down our equipment, then play from 12:30 to 3 in Masontown; the crowd would follow us over. And at the time there weren't a whole lot of bands playing: Dave C and the Sharptones; Joey and the Continentals came a little later; Tom King and the Starfires before they became the Outsiders; then there were the Grasshoppers, with Benny Orr—poor kid, he died too young; then there was Richie and the Fortunes.

It was a great time in the local band thing because everybody got along great. Our first gig was at Luccioni's in Richmond Heights, and on St. Clair we played at Leo's Café, on 75th and St. Clair, a blue-collar bar owned by a guy named Harry Veneri, the head of the union at Bowman Products on 72nd right off the freeway, an automotive parts warehouse. I worked there for a year after John Carroll. **—Steve Popovich, musician (Ronnie and the Savoys, the Twilighters)**

In addition to such bands as Dave C and the Sharptones on the West Side, Joey and the Continentals, and Bocky and the Visions on the East Side, there were girl singers like the Secrets ("The Boy Next Door") and Andrea Carroll ("Please Don't Talk to the Lifeguard"). Glenn Schwartz, who would later play in the Pilgrims, the James Gang, and Pacific Gas & Electric, was working with Frank Samson and the Wailers. La Cave opened in 1952; Leo's Casino moved uptown in 1963 (it was originally located at East 49th Street and Central Avenue; after a fire there, it moved to the Quad Hall hotel at 75th and Euclid and finally closed in 1972).

Kenny Margolis was practicing keyboards in Orange, preparing to form the Rebel Kind. Lost Soul Denny Carleton was cutting his teeth on Beatles riffs. Choir mainspring and future Raspberry Wally Bryson was attending Griswold Institute with Dan Gray, who wasn't quite Daffy yet; both were sent there for refusing to cut their hair. Cleveland's rock culture was bubbling under big.

SOUL AND SWEETNESS: Bocky and the Visions were a soul group who did major business in the '60s behind such local hits as "I Go Crazy"; the Poni-Tails scored nationally with "Born Too Late."

> The Cleveland music scene in the late '60s was fantastic. It was really unbelievable, the level of talent. You had the James Gang, with Joe Walsh and Jimmy Fox; you had the Choir, too; Wally had left and was already in Cyrus Erie with me; there were guys like Phil Giallombardo, a keyboardist [late Choir, early James Gang]; there was Joe Vitale's band down in Kent, the Measles. I used to drive down to J.B.'s, the club where the Raspberries ended up playing, just to watch him play; this was crazed, like jazz—he'd have this crazy rhythm going and then he'd just start to sing a lead, and it was like, wow. He played keyboards as well.

"Joe Walsh was as good then as he is now. You would walk into a place and there's a guy playing who's kind of the level of Jeff Beck—in a local Hullabaloo."

> Then you had Glass Harp with Phil Keaggy and Danny Pecchio. Phil Keaggy was an amazing guitar player. Between Cyrus Erie, the Choir, and the James Gang here in our town, and this other little periphery of things going on in Kent, there were some really great musicians playing around local clubs. Joe Walsh was as good then as he is now. You would walk into a place and there's a guy playing who's kind of the level of Jeff Beck—in a local Hullabaloo. And Wally as well; Wally's a phenomenal Pete Townshend–style guitar player. —**Eric Carmen, musician (Cyrus Erie, Quick, the Raspberries, solo)**

POOR GIRLS STRIKE IT RICH:

Way before the Runaways, the Poor Girls were an all-girl Akron act who opened for the likes of Cream and Steppenwolf. They were so popular they became a feature subject for the *Plain Dealer*'s Jane Scott. From left in the basement shot, that's Pam Johnson, Debbie Smith, Esta Johnson (standing), and Sue Schmidt.

The Poor Girls were an all-girl rock band in the mid-'60s who played around Akron and Kent and won coveted media attention when Jane Scott profiled them in the *Plain Dealer*. They opened for Cream at Akron Civic Theatre; they opened for Steppenwolf, too. Susan Schmidt-Horning, the lead vocalist, and Debbie Smith, the guitarist, who would later form the Akron underground group Chi-Pig, finish each other's sentences.

"The first gig we played out as the Poor Girls was Balauns' Family Restaurant, and we wore granny dresses because we're talking 1965, 1966, and the granny dress was very big. We went in there with our little Fender Vibro Champ amps and Esta (Esta Kerr and Pam Johnson were the other Poor Girls) had a good drum set, a Slingerland," Deb says. Sue adds, "The first gig we played in a club was with the Measles in the Outer Limits in Brimfield Plaza."

"Ravenna-Kentish, you don't want to go there," says Deb.

"The best thing about this gig is we go in there with our little Vibro Champ amps," Sue recalls, and Deb says, "We would plug our guitars in and Joe Walsh said uh-uh, you're using our equipment. He was lovely."

> The Saxons played a teen fair at Chippewa Lake Park in 1966 with the Measles, Joe Walsh's band before he joined the Gang. We're all sitting out on the porch one Saturday morning at Chippewa. It was way out on the southwest side of town, past Valley City. And we hear somebody doing a four-part version of "If I Needed Someone" by the Beatles. Me, the drummer, and the two guitar players are going, "Who the hell's that?" We left the cabin, went up the hill, went into the ballroom, it was Walsh with the Measles.
> **—Peanuts, fan (Fairview Park)**

Top 40 radio was the norm and WHK, WIXY, and Windsor, Ontario's CKLW set the pace, playing all kinds of music, even local stuff like Dick Whittington's Cats, the group led by Richie (of Richie and the Fortunes) Green. Credit a great promotion man:

> Roger Karshner was responsible for the Outsiders. By then, he was through with the Outsiders and looking for a new project. Our attorney had told him about us, so he came out and heard us at a place called the Sands in Portage Lakes, south of Akron. He liked it, said, "I've got an independent label with national promotion through Amy-Bell"—his label was called Round Records. He said, "I like the way you do 'Midnight Hour'; I'm going to rearrange it, we're going to call the band Dick Whittington's Cats." We said, "Why?" He said, "Because I have some promo ideas." So it was take it or

The Dick Whittington's Cats version of Wilson Pickett's "In the Midnight Hour" was a regional hit, but so many other versions competed against it, it didn't break out of the Midwest. The Cats were (from left), Richard Green, Buddy Maver, Terry McLeod, Tony Bodanza, and Jay Mohler.

leave it. We had nothing going, said we'd take it. We get in the studio, Cleveland Recording, at 14th and Euclid, and Chuck Mangione rearranged it and made it commercial. It was top ten in thirty-five markets. We didn't make a penny off the record but we got to do *Upbeat,* things like that, which is pretty cool at that age, to have that success.

"We didn't make a penny off the record but we got to do 'Upbeat'."

Dick Whittington was a mayor of London in the sixteenth century. What did that have to do with us? Nothing, as far as I can tell. The only thing Roger controlled was in the studio; we wanted to be an authentic R&B act even though we were white because that's what we loved, and he wanted to make it more of a pop situation. As far as success, he knew what he was doing. Probably wouldn't have worked the way we wanted it. He showed me this one letter he had sent to a radio station, along with a copy of the record and what looked like a cat's whisker. The note said, "Here's one of Dick Whittington's Cats' whiskers. Give it some play and next time we'll send you some pussy." —**Richard Green, musician (Richie and the Fortunes)**

Sonny Geraci, the voice of Tom King and the Starfires, the Outsiders, and Climax, has a story about the Outsiders:

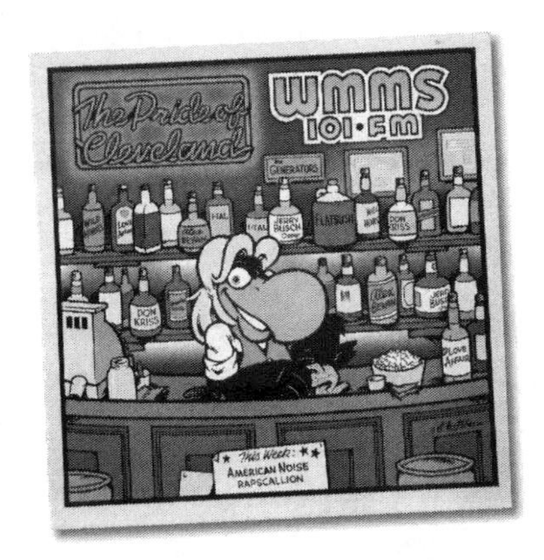

The big radio stations were KYC, WHK. I know for us to get played, Roger told them this is a new group, this is the biggest group on Capitol, they're from the West Coast. That's how we got played in Cleveland; if they had known it was Tom King & the Starfires, we would never have gotten played. Cleveland doesn't push their own people; never did. Roger Karshner was a genius at promoting. Capitol Records was owned by EMI; EMI's all over the world, when we were signed, we thought they'd put it out right away. They put it out in January; we started preparing to be stars. Wherever EMI had offices, Roger would have letters sent from there to all the program directors in America, the top stations. The first thing they're going to open up is something from France or Germany, all it would have was a sheet saying the Outsiders are coming. This went on for a couple of months, so by the time our record came out, they were pretty interested. When it finally came out, it started to take off in Cleveland and Pittsburgh, and when it broke in Baltimore, Capitol knew they had a hit. They put all their guns behind it and it took off. —**Sonny Geraci, musician (Tom King and the Starfires, the Outsiders, and Climax)**

Cleveland Flexes Its Musical Muscles

While Dick Whittington's Cats had their moment in the sun and the Outsiders reached number five in 1966 with "Time Won't Let Me," the big local acts were the James Gang, the Raspberries, and Michael Stanley, both as head of the Michael Stanley Band and on his own. The key Gang was Jim Fox, drummer and founder; Dale Peters, bassist; and Joe Walsh, guitarist and vocalist. Fox was in Richie and the Fortunes and the Outsiders before he founded the Gang in 1967:

GOING NATIONWIDE:

The Outsiders' great single, "Time Won't Let Me," went to number five nationally in 1966 thanks to Roger Karshner's wily promotion—and the strength of the song.

As the James Gang, we played the Hullabaloos more than any other band, I would venture to say. We played with the Yardbirds at the Mentor Hullabaloo; Joe was in the band, so it would have to be '68, '69, and the opening act was John Paul Jones and the American Navy. [Jones would soon join Led Zeppelin, the successor to the Yardbirds.] What I remember about John Paul Jones and the American Navy is that they had a male and female road crew, husband and wife roadies. We were more interested in talking to Page, Jimmy was always wonderful, the Yardbirds were the headliner, it was a packed house. —**Jimmy Fox, musician (the James Gang)**

There were different strata of players in town, like December's Children and the James Gang. December's

Children was the Balzer Brothers with Tommy Rich, and a band called the Dark Side used to play the Giant Tiger, a discount store like Uncle Bill's at West 140th and Lorain. Every Saturday afternoon they had a live band, the Dark Side or December's Children. The biggest thing in Cleveland that happened to me was the Teen Fair. I think that was at Public Hall, '67 or '68—or '69. Some music store locally had provided a bunch of drums, and right before the James Gang was going to play, one of the road crew went to another stage and grabbed a second bass drum; so everybody else played on a small drum set, but Jim Fox played on a double drum set—so they won the battle of the bands at Teen Fair. It was Glenn Schwartz. —**Dale Flanigan, musician (Dragonwyck)**

THE JAMES GANG STICKS IT TO YA:

No slouches at promotion, the James Gang used business cards and tattoos to make sure their fans remembered them.

"The biggest thing in Cleveland that happened to me was the Teen Fair."

Michael Stanley, who was in a group called Silk at that time, might have been there.

There used to be this thing called the Teen Fair in the basement of Public Hall, tied in with the *Plain Dealer* or the *Press,* and there would be teen fashion shows, and all day long, WIXY, the big Top 40 station, would bring people in like Andy Kim or Bobby Vee. I remember the last year before they got their deal the James Gang won the battle of the bands at the Teen Fair. Courtney Johns, our leader, wouldn't let us be in battles of the bands because he didn't want to risk losing, so we ended up backing a national artist or playing at the fashion show. —**Michael Stanley, musician (Silk, the Michael Stanley Band)**

Cyrus Erie set attendance records at the Chesterland Hullabaloo and the Mentor Hullabaloo.

The Rebel Kind and the Mods kept intersecting, there were also the Lost Souls [with Denny Carleton, later in the Choir]; the Damnation of Adam Blessing played a few times at the armories; and there was the James Gang. The first time I saw them it was Glenn Schwartz and Jimmy Fox and Phil Giallombardo was playing organ with them. Glenn was the one who really blew everybody away, even more so than the Mods, who came in and really did a number on everybody with vocal harmonies. Then we saw Glenn Schwartz; he was older, but he played guitar like Jimi Hendrix. Nobody knew anything about how to play like that, to do vibrato on the guitar, stretch the strings, it was like, what is that? And the semi-distortion he was getting; the Mods didn't do that either, it was always very straight, clean guitar. That would have been early '67. —**Ken Margolis (musician, the Rebel Kind, the Choir)**

While the James Gang was settling into its classic lineup of Fox, bassist Dale Peters, and guitarist Joe Walsh, the Choir was ruling the Hullabaloo scene, along with Cyrus Erie and the Quick. Eventually, they would come together in the Raspberries, perhaps the most successful Cleveland group.

The lure of a storied bass player beckoned Eric Carmen, the voice of the Sounds of Silence, Cyrus Erie, and the Quick. But let's not get ahead of ourselves. When Carmen first heard of Dave Burke, he was attending high school and had just formed his first real group, the Sounds of Silence.

SMALL HANDS, LARGE TALENT:

The Choir's Wally Bryson (second from left) absorbed guitar magic wherever he could, including a Byrds concert in Painesville.

Rumor had filtered from the far east of Mentor and Painesville all the way to Brush High School in Lyndhurst about the Squire, so one day Marty Murphy and I decided to venture forth out of Lyndhurst to Painesville Armory, which to us was like going to Africa. We had to see what the fuss was about. We got out there—we were just old enough to drive—and we walked into this armory and there was the Choir. Dave Smalley, Jim Bonfanti, Dan Klawon (he and Jim would switch off as drummers), and Dave Burke, the Squire. And here was Wally Bryson on a Rickenbacker twelve-string playing "Substitute" by the Who, "Look Through Any Window" by the Hollies, and they all had cool long hair.

Dave Burke was unbelievable. He was just the fastest—he was like an idiot savant. Where everybody else was playing dum dum dum, Dave Burke was running up and down his bass like Duck Dunn in Memphis. He was amazing. If you listen to "It's Cold Outside," the bass is flying all over the record. Needless to say, we were blown away. We were blown away with the whole band, and the minute I saw Wally on that stage, I knew I had to get in a band with this guy. —**Eric Carmen, musician**

> **"We decided to venture forth out of Lyndhurst to Painesville Armory, which to us was like going to Africa."**

Wally Bryson had animal magnetism for sure.

In the fall of 1967, Maple Heights High consisted of two cultural groups, the collegiates and the greasers. They were in some ways similar to England's mods and rockers but there was a difference. Mods and rockers were both working-class kids. Greasers, at least at Maple, were, more often than not, ethnic (Italians, Hungarians, et cetera) while collegiates were more WASPish. Also, greasers came from the working class and were more likely to study "trade-type" classes such as wood and metal shop. They were also the more violent of the two. Collegiates were more upper class. The two groups didn't really dislike each other, they simply didn't associate. There was also a small group of emerging hippies. They were disliked by the school administration, greasers, and collegiates alike. This brings us to the Maple Heights Fall Homecoming of 1967. Two bands were playing at the time: the Strangers, which featured a stunning twelve-year-old drummer named Billy Greer, and, headlining, the Choir, which had a huge Cleveland hit at the time, "It's Cold Outside."

SUITED FOR ACTION:
The Raspberries strike a power pop pose.

"The greasers were really unhappy that the Choir, which they considered a bunch of long-haired sissies, were playing their dance."

The greasers were really unhappy that the Choir, which they considered a bunch of long-haired sissies, were playing their dance. I suspect they would have been much happier with one of their own groups like [Buddy Maver's] Charade or the Sensations. The rude comments and shout-outs began as the Choir played. The catcalls continued and the greasers began tossing pennies at the band. After one particular song concluded, Wally, with that cocky smile, motioned one of the offenders to the front of the stage. The kid and his friends fearlessly sauntered up. What harm could these sissies possibly bring to them? As soon as the greasers reached the front of the stage, Wally unstrapped his guitar and swung it upside the head of the nearest greaser. The Choir grabbed Wally and ran out the fire exit at the rear of the stage. Everyone emptied into the streets. Wally's action was the single most inspirational act of bravado/craziness I had witnessed up until that time. I've never forgotten it. —**Mitch Renko, fan (Euclid)**

I had just gotten this brand-new Gibson twelve-string, it's the first gig I'm playing it on. Maple Heights wasn't into the longhair scene, some kid was tossing nickels at the band, it was really pissing me off. This kid was bouncing pennies and nickels off of my guitar, so I finally spotted him. In between songs, I went to the microphone and said, "Hey you, you're a punk." He came walking to the stage like he was going to kick my ass. I let him get halfway into his climb and conked him on the side of the head with my new guitar I was so worried about. Then I jumped off the stage, we wrassled around. His mother called me the next day and asked me to pay for his sweater that got ripped. I said, "Hey lady, he was putting nicks into my $350 guitar, you want to pay for that?" **—Wally Bryson, musician (the Choir, the Raspberries)**

The early '70s also was an amazing time, even for exclusively local bands. Recalls one former East Side drummer, who named his first group the Buddy Cosmo Band:

We used to play schools like St. Ann's, St. Jerome's, high school dances, St. Paschal Baylon on Wilson Mills, Beaumont. We were hired for their dances; we used to have mixers in the high school or grade school gym. These were bands like us, Eastwind, and the Raspberries. It was $1. I'll tell you who else used to play at St. Ann's all the time: Glass Harp, with Phil Keaggy and Danny Pecchio. I used to see the North River Street Rock Collection; Jamey Haddad was the drummer in that band . . . We were freshmen at Cathedral Latin when the James Gang played there for a dance. It was like a mixer. Joe Walsh, Dale Peters, and Jimmy Fox. It was phenomenal. **—Vince Malatesta, fan (South Euclid)**

As the '60s slipped into the '70s, the single began to lose ground to the LP, FM took over from AM, and rock went corporate. The James Gang and the Raspberries mounted major tours and scored modest radio hits. It would be up to Michael Stanley to define what Cleveland rock is about, frustrations and all—and to set attendance records at Blossom and the Coliseum. Stanley grew up on the West Side and worked in the Sceptres and the Tree Stumps (aka Silk) before he recorded his first solo album. He recalls that Silk once played "at a place called the Note, in Ruggles Beach, between Lorain and Cedar Point."

I can remember we were playing with the Kingsmen, which I thought was the coolest thing in the world. [The Kingsmen made history with "Louie, Louie."] I remember being out back of the club and the drummer for the Kingsmen came out, and we were talking and he offers me a joint. It's the first time I've ever heard, seen, or come across something like this. I think it's like heroin—I can't do this, if I take a hit of this I would become an ax murderer. I abstained.

The first show we did was at the Syrian Mosque in Pittsburgh, this would have been about '69—we opened for Blood, Sweat & Tears, the David Clayton Thomas version. We're standing in the wings at this proscenium theater and I remember the guy coming to us saying, "I'm going to give you the high sign and all you guys walk out in the dark, get your instruments on, I'll introduce you, the lights will go on, and bam, go!"

FEELING RIGHT AT HOME: **MSB Rocks a favorite venue: The Agora.**

As we start to walk onstage for our first major concert appearance in our history, the first guy trips, falls down, and everybody falls on top of him in a huge pile. And they turned the lights on. It looked like we were at a rush party at a gay frat house. I remember thinking it can only get better from here on. We played. I remember nothing about it whatsoever. The next day, at Kent State, we opened for Sly and the Family Stone and Country Joe and the Fish. We did about six shows with Sly, and I think the best he did was an hour and a half late. I remember one show in Dayton or Columbus where we were supposed to go on first, he says, "I'll open for you." It was like, well, dude, no one's going to be here. You're who they came to see. —**Michael Stanley, musician (Silk, the Michael Stanley Band)**

"It looked like we were at a rush party at a gay frat house."

Things got better:

We weren't that unapproachable type of rock band. We didn't wear Spandex. The guys in the band were just a bunch of talented, regular people. No one looked down on the audience; we just happened to work harder, longer, and maybe got luckier. I remember one night at Blossom—one of those sell-outs, it really rained, the parking lots were swamped—half the guys in the band went out after we played a three-and-a-half-hour show and put ropes on their trucks and pulled people out of the mud. There were some of the first four-wheel-drive things I've ever seen, and they're pulling people out of the mud at two o'clock in the morning so these sixteen-year-old girls don't get murdered by their parents when they get home. It was that thing of, hey, show's over, it's back to the real world, and this was the real world. I don't want to play with people who don't have that feeling. —**Michael Stanley**

Stage Pass and *Friends and Legends*

I've been managing Michael Stanley for—it has to be thirty years. What was most memorable in my mind was when we sold out four days of Blossom. To this day, that record stands. It was an incredible feat by Michael and the band to do that. This was like history being made, and it was exciting knowing that I was helping get it to that point. It was a wonderful part of my career, without question. Michael is a first-class, honorable, loyal individual. At Blossom, people were standing for the whole show, people were rushing the stage. It was something that no one could ever forget. —**Mike Belkin, promoter**

The band set several attendance records, including 21,500 at the Richfield Coliseum on New Year's Day 1982, and 66,377 over four nights at Blossom Music Center in 1982. That Blossom sellout string, August 25, 26, 30, and 31, was their grand slam, topping the previous Blossom record—also set by MSB, the year before. On September 29, 1984, the group drew 76,000 to the Municipal Stadium parking lot.

"Michael Stanley was the Beatles in the late '70s, early '80s. Michael Stanley is still our biggest-selling artist ever, by far. He was probably the most talented artist not to make it out of Cleveland. It was a Midwest sound, just straight rock and roll. " —**Greg Beaumont, owner of the Record Den**

My fave local performer is Michael Stanley because I like him personally and because he's a survivor. That's a true Clevelander for ya. A hardworking survivor against all odds kind of guy. —**Janet Macoska, photographer**

Local has its limitations:

The worst thing to happen to any band is to actually be popular locally. Look at X in L.A. Certainly the rule applies here; Michael Stanley held the record at Blossom Music Center and couldn't draw 300 people in Detroit. But a situation like that also indicates that there's something wrong in this music scene. If we have a guy who's a superstar here but nobody else in the world knows him, it means that either we're stifling him or our standards are sub par. —**Mark Addison, musician (the Generators, A Nation of One, the Borrowers)**

We weren't stars, you know what I mean? We were that Midwestern thing, Seger and all those people, and Mellencamp, which is fine musically. But they lumped all those together, and they're not . . . we don't all do the same thing.

We couldn't get arrested in LA. Did great in San Francisco. When we were selling 90,000 seats up here, we were lucky to sell 3,000 in Columbus. What's the difference? Here, you couldn't turn on the radio without being subjected to us one way or another. When MMS was behind you, it worked. We played a lot of free shows for them when they got going. But we got a little bigger, we were almost so big that they couldn't have complete control over the situation. They could pretty much tell anybody what to do. Leo would interview me, play one side of the album, interview me some more, play the other side of the album. When's the last time you heard a whole-album play? That's what radio was. Back then, Leo might be playing two different tracks, Denny might be playing another track. You might have seven, eight tracks on the frigging radio. —**Michael Stanley, musician**

"You couldn't turn on the radio without being subjected to us one way or another."

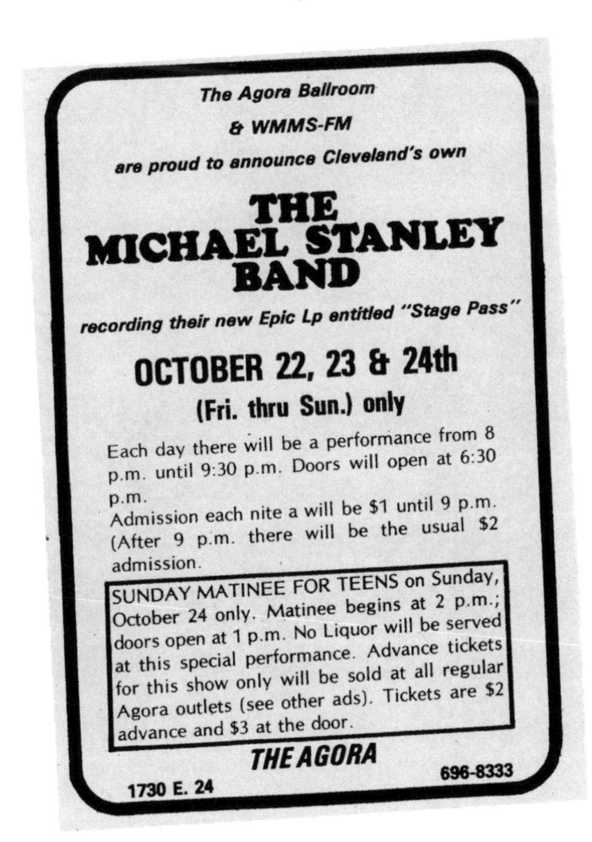

The Agora Ballroom
& WMMS-FM
are proud to announce Cleveland's own

THE MICHAEL STANLEY BAND

recording their new Epic Lp entitled "Stage Pass"

OCTOBER 22, 23 & 24th
(Fri. thru Sun.) only

Each day there will be a performance from 8 p.m. until 9:30 p.m. Doors will open at 6:30 p.m.
Admission each nite a will be $1 until 9 p.m. (After 9 p.m. there will be the usual $2 admission.

SUNDAY MATINEE FOR TEENS on Sunday, October 24 only. Matinee begins at 2 p.m.; doors open at 1 p.m. No Liquor will be served at this special performance. Advance tickets for this show only will be sold at all regular Agora outlets (see other ads). Tickets are $2 advance and $3 at the door.

THE AGORA
1730 E. 24
696-8333

The Numbers Band circa 1973. From left: Drake Gleason (bass), Jay Brown (drums), and brothers Jack Kidney and Bob Kidney

IN THE TRENCHES

Other Local Acts

Consider all those bands that could've/should've but just couldn't/didn't make it big. Some came close. Many had strong followings. Others had moments of glory, maybe, but moments only.

In the late '60s and early '70s, the Damnation of Adam Blessing released four albums (the last under the name Glory) on a major label. The band had professional management, a big local following, even several local hits. But it couldn't quite go nationwide.

When I was with the Society, the band that turned into Damnation, there were battles of the bands. I remember us winning, and Jane Scott was there and invited us all down to her office and she did a big article on us. This has got to be '67; everybody listened to WIXY and the FMs were just coming in. That's where we met Eric Stevens, our producer. We were the house band at D'Poo's Tool and Dye Works, Dick Korn's club in the Flats. Eric Stevens was down there one night, he goes, you guys want to make a record?

It happened so fast. Eric's dad was a very, very powerful independent record promoter. His dad—Perry Stevens—made a phone call to United Artists Records, it probably went something like this: Hey, my kid wants to make a record, he's got this band, Damnation of Adam Blessing. The president probably said okay, let him make a record and we'll send you the money. I'm telling you, Perry made a phone call; they never heard us and they released our first album, which went to number one in Cleveland, stayed up there for eleven weeks, the single "Morning Dew," the first cut on the album.
—Jim Quinn, musician (the Society, the Damnation of Adam Blessing)

I was at D'Poo's Tool and Dye Works, a little flatiron building down in the Flats, and Damnation played the bar; that's where I found Alex Bevan, too. This was at the mid- to end of 1969; I think I discovered them about a month before I left WIXY. I thought they were a fit for what was really happening at that time, and that there was some good musicianship and vocals.

DAMNATION SOARING: The Damnation of Adam Blessing did so well in the area it became a local legend. But it couldn't spread its heavy rock word nationwide.

Northeast Ohio Bands and Performers Who Made Their Mark in the 1960s

15 60 75 / The Numbers Band
Audi Badoo
Backwoodsmen
Baskerville Hounds
Blackwelles
Bocky and the Visions
Andrea Carroll
The Case of E.T. Hooley
The Choir ("It's Cold Outside")
Chylds
City Squires
Cyrus Erie ("Get the Message")
Damnation of Adam Blessing ("Morning Dew")
Dave C. and the Sharptones
Dave Griggs Blues Band
December's Children (previously known as Ambleside)
Dick Whittington's Cats
Euphrates
Frank Samson and the Wailers
Freeport Express
Glass Harp
Grasshoppers (with Ben Orr)
Hessler Court
James Gang
Jimmy Vince and the Proof Sets (later known as Mixed Emotions—Ben Orr was in both)
Joey and the Continentals (later the GTOs)
Kicks, Inc.
The Lost Souls
The Measles
The Mods
The Monarchs
Moses
Mr. Stress
Muther's Oats
North River Street Rock Collection
Occasions
The Outsiders
Paper Sun

And I liked some of the songs they were singing. It was in that zone of the second wave, after Cream and Hendrix. A lot of hit acts were very influenced by the Who and Cream and Hendrix and *Sgt. Pepper's*. They did something live, Hendrix's "You Got Me Floatin'," the kids would go nuts when they would do it.

I got them their first album on United Artists; my dad was an independent promotion man. The first single off the album did very well in Cleveland, "Morning Dew." Then United Artists got excited, we got them showcased at the Village Gate in New York, a club in Chicago, and the Whiskey A Go Go, a very hot club on the strip in Los Angeles. This is '70, '71. Wolfman Jack loved one of their songs, "New York City Woman."

There's a sense when you see an act and you watch the crowd. This is L.A., and Wolfman Jack loved them, but you could feel it in the club: it wasn't something that was going to blow these people away. That's not saying anything negative about the band; a baseball analogy would be somebody losing the World Series doesn't mean they're not a good team. That was a turning point; I still thought this was a terrific group, but they weren't blowing people away in those markets . . . Grand Funk Railroad produced a lot of records in the same studio—all of their first albums were produced at Cleveland Recording by Terry Knight. The point is that capturing those kinds of groups on record isn't as easy as it sounds, but when you play live in those venues, if you blow people away, it's going to happen one way or another. And Grand Funk just blew people away live. A song on the second Damnation album called "Back to the River" actually went to number one in a lot of smaller markets, but United Artists didn't do what's called in the business bringing the record home. **—Eric Stevens, promoter**

Damnation got airplay and press and drew very well. It was one of those bands that straddled AM and FM, when album rock came to the forefront—and long, long tunes with long, long solos. What of local bands like Dragonwyck that didn't reach that level, let alone the popularity of Cleveland's Big Three, the James Gang, Raspberries, and Michael Stanley?

Local Lights and the Underground

We were playing at Jicky's English Disco at 20-something and Euclid, it was the top of this hotel, and we'd finish at 2 or 2:30 in the morning . . . Swingos was at 18th. You'd finish and pretty much go there and hang out with whoever was in town. Tom Jones, Ian Hunter, Bowie, they'd all be there. I was playing in Dragonwyck at the time, this was '72, '73, and we played a lot of places downtown. It was cover tunes, but we did our originals, too. We played Procol Harum tunes, more of that artsy stuff: Moody Blues, the Doors. We did some nice show openers. We opened for the Bar-Kays at a place in Kent, Friar Tuck's or one of those, about a week or two before they went down. [Most of the Bar-Kays died with Otis Redding in December 1967, the morning after they'd backed him on *Upbeat* and at Leo's Casino.]

"Whoever was playing in town would go to the bar at Swingos."

Whoever was playing in town would go to the bar at Swingos. They were sitting there and you'd go up and say hi, I enjoyed the show or I missed the show because I had a gig that night. There was something else happening that was very Clevelandish. There were a lot of after-hours places to go to and a lot of people lived downtown. A guy named Basil used to live on Prospect or Huron and had a party on the roof of his building and the police came, this was '72, there were probably 300 people all over the roof and in the apartment and somebody yelled be quiet, the police are outside. And this drunk girl said, "What happened?" And she swung and her elbow hit his picture window and all the glass broke and fell down on the hood of the cruiser. And within minutes there must have been thirty cruisers there, and we were hiding on the roof, everybody was drunk, smoking pot and having sex, all the things we were doing back then.

I'll never forget watching the glass go down on the cruiser in slow motion. We had played at a place called the Clockwork Orange on Prospect; this was an after-hours party at Basil Santana's. He was a Hispanic guy who was into Latin music when we were all into hard rock. In the middle of his living room he had a drum set and we'd bang on his drums. He was a very nice guy and a fantastic drummer. Now it's all in the suburbs; there's not a lot downtown unless it's investment bankers buying up condos that are investments by Wolstein. It was wonderful. We played a job and then we went to that party.

—Dale Flanigan, musician (Dragonwyck)

By 1975, when stadium shows were common and bands sold millions, a vocal minority began wanting to hear different sounds and there were groups to oblige. In the late '70s, the underground mutated into punk and its better-tailored relative, new wave. Cleveland and Akron were breeding grounds for both. The Agora was often ground zero:

Penny Arcade
The Poor Girls
The Quick
Reactions
Richie and the Fortunes
Robert Lockwood Jr.
Ronnie and the Savoys
The Saxons
The Scovils
The Sounds of Silence
Speedometer
Statesmen
The Strangers
Symphonics
Tiffany Shade
Tom King & the Starfires
Tree Stumps (turned into Silk, featuring Michael Stanley)
Twilighters
White Wolf Drake

DRUM GOD:

Former Dragonwyck drummer Dale Flanigan, caught in a promotional pose.

Home for Christmas 1978, I caught note of a show scheduled at the Agora—a twin bill of northern Ohio bands: Devo and the Dead Boys.

I can close my eyes and smell the sweaty, smoky, acrid stench of a packed nightclub on a very cold night . . . Devo blew the place away. Now *here* was art rock . . . Dressed in their classic flowerpot hats and industrial yellow jumpsuits . . . Mark Mothersbaugh at one point sang from a playpen laid out on the plastic-covered stage. And then: The Dead Boys. Dark, glowering, focused like a razor, they came out and proceeded to pump through the material on *Young, Loud and Snotty.* No politics, no socialism, just furious Stooge-like energy and a sound like bombs exploding onstage.

These weren't disaffected New York art intellectuals; no sir. These were Cleveland boys. The only thing they were serious about was wringing every possible watt out of their Marshall stacks. And they weren't pretty, either. Jimmy Zero looked just like the kind of guy every mother was terrified that her daughter would come home with, cigarette dangling dangerously from the corner of his mouth, half in, half out of the dark. Cheetah equally menacing, Johnny "Blitz" Madansky literally thuglike . . .

And Stiv Bators. As in command of that small stage as Mick Jagger had ever been of any stage, anywhere. At the end of the last encore, he pulled his trick. Looping the microphone up over a beam in the low Agora ceiling, he then wrapped its cord around his neck and proceeded to hoist all (maybe) 120 pounds of himself into the air. Yes, he was hanging. *For real*? We can never know, though his roadie seemed to panic and rushed to cut the cord and bring him down.

Maybe *not* real . . . He had enough presence of mind to conclude the act by dropping his drawers and thrusting his skinny ass to the audience, balls dangling, and a schlong that was surprisingly big waving between his bony knees.

This was punk, Cleveland style. Brutal, humorous, unpretentious, apolitical. —**Paul Nickels, fan (Lakewood)**

A DEVASTATING DOUBLE BILL:

The Dead Boys and Devo made the 1977 Christmas season one to remember when they played the Agora in one of the rare pure underground shows there.

I remember going to see Rocket from the Tombs at the Viking Saloon and thinking the band was really, really amazing but I had no designs on trying to join the band. Peter Laughner had given me his parents' piano, which [today] is here in New York, four blocks from here.

I was driving a van down Cedar Avenue, Peter was in the back beating the

IMPRESSIVE IN MORE WAYS THAN ONE:

Stiv Bators sure knew how to make a spectacle of himself—and rock his ass off while he was doing it.

crap out of the piano, singing Velvets' songs. I had the piano in my apartment and Peter started coming over to my house all the time. I remember once he goes, man, I just heard this guy, you're not going to believe this, he starts pounding on the piano, started screaming this song, "I Came for You," by this guy Bruce Springsteen. Peter was so funny, he was singing it like Bob Dylan. —**Tony Maimone, musician (Pere Ubu)**

The initial punk rock years were a great time for live rock and roll in Cleveland. As an inveterate Agora attendee circa 1974 to 1980—I'd just go there without even checking to see who was playing—I once stumbled upon one of the few live performances of Cleveland's legendary Rocket from the Tombs. Now for a guy whose idea of great music at the time was progressive rock, à la Yes, this was quite a shock . . . Glowering in the dark, Peter Laughner was throwing off metal shards while the rotund David "Crocus Behemoth" Thomas bellowed like a sheep in the process of being castrated, THIS was something different . . . And a hint of what was to come.

RFTT wasn't in it for the long haul, but over the next couple of years, its bastard stepchildren—the Dead Boys and Pere Ubu—provided a lot of riveting moments. I particularly recall descending the stairs to the Pop Shop, a place where bands that couldn't fill the Agora upstairs could work their thing out, and being frontally assaulted by the same David

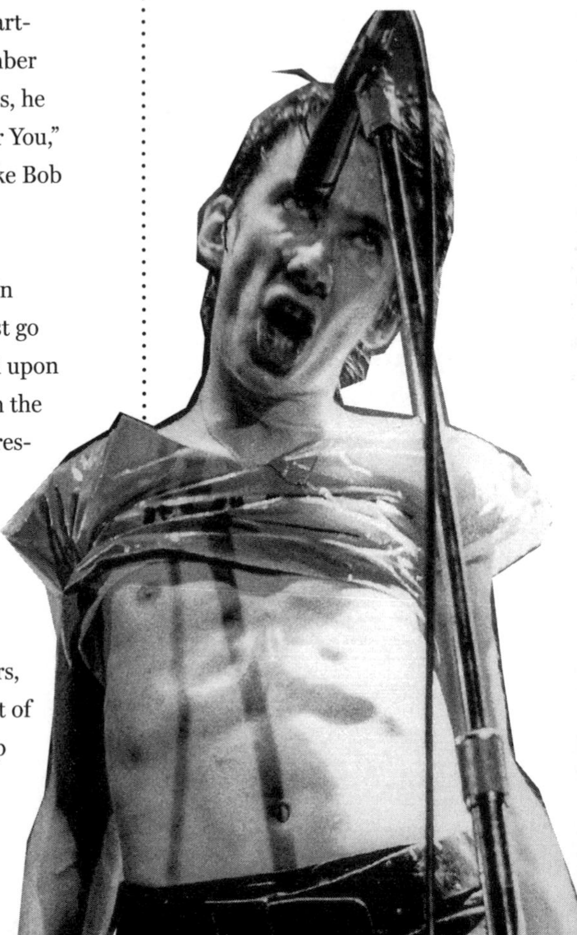

PUNK AND NEW WAVE BUBBLE UNDER:

The late '70s and early '80s were a rich time for the underground, with clubs like Hennessy's and the Agora showcasing subversive local talent.

Thomas and his industrial machine, Pere Ubu. Thomas was bleating and banging a block of wood with a hammer. It was absolutely fucking riveting, and it was real art, springing right from the grimy streets of our dying town. —**Paul Nickels**

"It was real art, springing right from the grimy streets of our dying town."

If you went to Los Angeles in '77, the punk scene wasn't much bigger. There are more photographs that remain of the bands that were around in '77 in L.A. The thing that's funny is the music that came out of that pretty much became the mainstream by 1990, so when these kids in the late '90s or this century want to go back to discover the punk scene they have this impression there was this thing going on that was this huge revolution in music. The truth is, yeah, musically speaking I think it was a big shift, but the actual cultural phenomenon went by almost unnoticed except for the 300 of us in every city who thought it was like, everything. But it just came and went and it is well documented, so that's why everybody today looks back . . . MTV won't tell you about Cleveland or Detroit, but they'll tell you about New York or L.A. But really it was the same kind of thing. —**John Thompson, former record store owner and promoter**

The gatekeeper to the underground was David Thomas. Before he took over Ubu from Peter Laughner, he wrote for *Scene* as Crocus Behemoth; he also worked as doorman at the Viking Saloon. He embodied the sound of the strange and still runs Ubu, Cleveland's most influential underground band. The incubator for Ubu, Cleveland's best-known underground band, was the Plaza, 3206 Prospect Avenue.

The Plaza was an art project, it was never a commune, it was just a place for basically everybody to live and people to play music. There were no problems with volume and everybody was into downtown. Everybody else was told, don't go downtown and if you made it to downtown Cleveland, don't go to Prospect. And when we were playing in the Flats, everybody said, don't go down in the Flats, especially at night. This was when we started playing at the Pirate's Cove, in '75 maybe. It became Peabody's Down Under. Tony mentioned to me they had a bunch of free nights open; apparently Friday and Saturday nights were huge but the rest of the week was weaker. Jim Dowd was the owner, so Tony said if you have some extra nights, we have a band, so he was like, what kind of band? Do you guys play Rolling Stones? Tony said no, we play original music.

What happened was that we convinced Jim to let us play there. He had nothing to lose and everything to gain. The first two Tuesday nights, a handful of people showed up. Then we said, hey, we've got a better idea. Let's move it to Thursday because it's closer to the weekend and everybody has only one day of work left, and everybody can struggle through it. Let's make it like a pre-weekend thing, so we did that for about a year, and he was happy. Tin Huey came up and Devo came up, and the Nerves came through, and all these other bands were coming through and the crowds were, like, pretty steady; the place only packed 250 in, that was not a big club.
—R. Scott Krauss, musician (Pere Ubu)

"When we were playing in the Flats, everybody said, don't go down in the Flats, especially at night."

The first tour Ubu did was '78. "We only did five or six shows," recalls Krauss. "We called that thing the Coed Jail Tour. We went out on the road; we tasted the mass success of the whole rock and roll monster."

Crocus was a huge figure on stage, he might be doing something simple as having a hammer and a big railroad spike, clanking along with a 4/4 beat on something like "Final Solution" or "30 Seconds over Tokyo"; they were a lot more fun to watch than bands who were really into progressive rock, like Yes and Emerson, Lake & Palmer. And I wasn't really into, like, the Eagles or a lot of the singer-songwriters that were popular around that time on radio. MMS was a big part of the stuff, with playing David Bowie, Lou Reed, New York Dolls, Sensational Alex Harvey Band, Springsteen obviously. **—Chris Jacobs, fan (Rocky River)**

As for underground shows in the Flats, "it was never a packed scene," says Jacobs. "You'd kind of recognize some of the same faces who were following the band and watching them. But there were times a little later on, after Ubu started committing some things to vinyl, when the crowds were getting a little bigger."

CROCUS IN CONTROL: David Thomas ruled the room with Pere Ubu.

Reading *Scene* magazine I learned about Crocus Behemoth, David Thomas. If you paid close attention, you'd read about Rocket from the Tombs, all these exotic bands. I didn't see Rocket; the band that caught our fancy—and we were old enough at that time, just eighteen—was Pere Ubu, and that sort of brought us into the whole world of Ubu and learning about the Drome and eventually things like the Dead Boys. In '76 and '77, I was away at Miami of Ohio, so over the summers and winters we started going to the Thursday nights at the Pirate's Cove, where Pere Ubu was playing. The two bands we were into in terms of local music were Wild Horses, because we thought they were a great covers band, and at the other end of the spectrum, it was Ubu. We were regulars at the Thursday night Pirate's Cove shows. There was a cool scene but it wasn't, like, packed. In the winter, it was so cold in there you couldn't put your feet on the ground for the entire show, it would be freezing. . . .

A DIFFERENT KIND OF CLEVELAND SOUND: Pere Ubu—that's David Thomas second to left—is the sound of the Rust Belt grinding to a halt. It's also the sound of something different, always different.

It didn't take a high IQ to understand the context of David Thomas standing there at Pirate's Cove pounding on an anvil. It sort of made sense when you walked outside and listened to the sounds of the barren industrial Flats, all the squeaks and squawks of the synthesizers. Music of isolation and desolation somehow all seemed to fit. It felt like you were in a special club, because it was way off the radar. We took pride in going to those Ubu shows. Sometimes they would be aggressively non-accessible music, but we always wanted to give it a shot. We knew something was going on, knew something was happening here, but didn't know what it was.

Between sets, we would climb out on these industrial structures and get high and look out at the Flats. Right across the street, there was a parking lot with this big steel structure and we would climb on it. —**Bob Burford, fan (Kent)**

"We knew something was going on, knew something was happening here, but didn't know what it was."

My Favorite Northeast Ohio Groups and Artists

by Michael Stanley, *musician, Michael Stanley Band*

1. The James Gang
2. O'Jays
3. Michael Stanley Band
4. Raspberries
5. Nine Inch Nails
6. Breathless
7. Levert
8. Cyrus Erie
9. The Case of E.T. Hooley
10. The Dazz Band

Ubu went on to worldwide tours, critical acclaim, and numerous musical and personality differences. Now, it's largely one of David Thomas's many brand extensions.

Another band with nearly as high a profile as Ubu and an even deeper legacy is the Numbers Band, the group Bob and Jack Kidney formed in Kent in 1970. They played all over the place, but Kent is where they made their stand.

The Erie Café was a dive on Water Street in Kent, right next to the Crane Street Bridge. I was still at Kent State University High School. I played there with my own band called City Lights; they had a go-go dancer who was well past her prime, and she wore a tiger-spotted bikini when she danced on the breaks, and she had stretch marks and she danced to a song called "Rub It In." One night all of the bikers were lined up listening to the band and they were into it. I tore down the equipment and I was the last one out, and they formed a circle around me in the parking lot and the smallest, punkiest one came up and started giving me a hard time while the other guys watched.

I thought I was going to get the shit kicked out of me by these guys, but then I told them they had just gotten through listening to me play, they had liked the band, I had played the harmonica, they seemed to like that. What did I do? And they apologized and backed off and patted me on the back and told me they were sorry. I was scared shitless; are you kidding? It was a cast of characters in there. Chris Butler played in the band. We played all blues, maybe a couple originals that weren't very original. It was summer of 1972.

I have another story from the Erie Café. Bob was playing at the Kove, and he got a bigger job or a better job or another job and canceled for the night, and the owner of the Kove called me at work—I was a bellman at the Hilton West on Market Street; Chrissie Hynde used to work there. He said, could I fill in for 15 60 75? [They weren't the Numbers Band then.] I jumped at the chance because they were packing the house and I knew I'd be playing for a really large audience. We were booked at the Erie Café that night, so I called the owner of the Erie Café and told him we couldn't play that night and he asked me why. I was seventeen. I told him that the drummer's mother had died. Well, it's right up the street from the Kove, within walking distance. A short walk.

So I'm playing and the owner of the Erie Café comes walking into the Kove, and he sat down in front of the band and I sang in front of the band and he showed me his gun and he was yelling at me and stuff. He left. He didn't shoot me. That was a Saturday night; I walked in Monday and apologized. —**Jack Kidney, musician (the Numbers Band)**

BY THE NUMBERS:

15 60 75 aka The Numbers Band worked Kent bars like no other group. Here, the group plays J.B.'s in 1977. From left to right: Chris Butler, bass; Robert Kidney, guitar; David Robinson, drums; Mike Stacey, guitar; Tim Magliore, congas; Terry Hynde, maracas; Jack Kidney, harmonica.

My Favorite Songs from Northeast Ohio Bands

by Michael Norman, *Cleveland Plain Dealer Arts Editor*

1. The Pretenders: "Precious"
2. Dead Boys/Rocket from the Tombs: "Ain't It Fun"
3. The Choir: "It's Cold Outside "
4. The Raspberries: "I Wanna Be with You"
5. Nine Inch Nails: "Down in It"
6. James Gang: "Funk #49"
7. The Outsiders: "Time Won't Let Me"
8. Pere Ubu/Rocket from the Tombs: "30 Seconds over Tokyo"
9. Glass Harp: "Look in the Sky"
10. Cobra Verde: "Crashing in a Plane"

Local support has helped the Numbers. Still does, particularly when guns (again) are involved:

We're back at Pancho Villa's, things are really fuckin' bleak, and the guy had promised us a certain amount of money and the manager did not pay us that money at the end of the week. So I went to the owner's house across the street from the bar, and he's hanging out with a bunch of the Cleveland Browns in his house, these giant guys. I knock on the door; he lets me in with these guys hanging out with him and I demand my money. And he put a gun on the table and told me I wasn't getting any more money. I didn't get the money. Then several months later I needed psychiatric help and went into a five-month depression. I couldn't wait until I could go to sleep and I hated to wake up. It was bad, it was real bad. I realized that this was not working out for me, that it just wasn't working out. **—Jack Kidney**

"I demand my money. And he put a gun on the table and told me I wasn't getting any more money. I didn't get the money."

TALK ABOUT A WORKING BAND:

Like many other northern Ohio bands, the Numbers worked all the time. Still do. The bars may die, but the Numbers live on.

I was considering quitting and Murray Saul [from MMS] showed up with Peter Laughner to see us play there one night. They were both really excited, I don't mean on speed. I went outside with Peter and said I'm really thinking about quitting. Peter said, "Would you do me a personal favor?" He said, "I want you to stick with this band, do it for three more months, and at the end of three months, if things aren't better, you should quit." Within that three-month period, J.B.'s reopened and they came down and gave us our job back and we played there for twenty years. **—Bob Kidney, musician (the Numbers Band)**

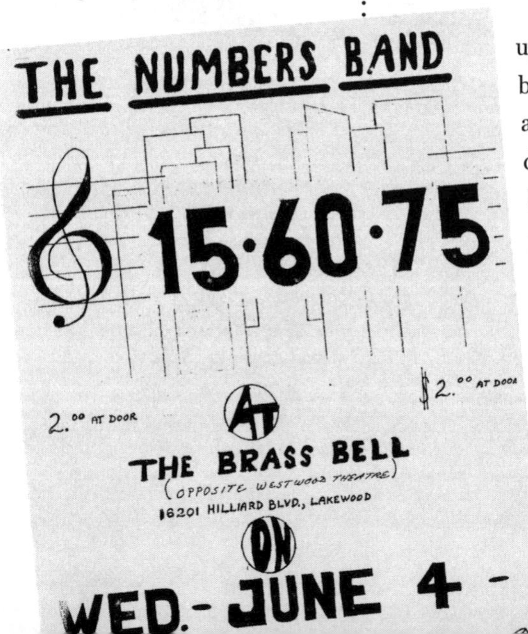

Riding the New Wave

Other bands, like Lucky Pierre and the Generators, had shorter, flashier careers.

Lucky Pierre, led by Lakewood talent Kevin McMahon, was between underground and mainstream.

> It was new wave, right when Elvis Costello broke, and Squeeze just came out with their first record. It was lifting off of the British-influenced pop stuff that came before, which was the Kinks and T. Rex. Pere Ubu kind of almost started as a joke with David Thomas and some of the other journalists; they used to play down by Cleveland State at the Viking Saloon when David performed under his pen name, Crocus Behemoth. There were a lot of punk things going on in Cleveland at the same time Iggy and the Stooges got started, like the Electric Eels, which was Kevin McMahon's brother's band . . . and they would just be as offensive and confrontational as you can imagine: swastikas onstage . . . almost like a performance art thing, but when you do it in a bar in front of people, it can get out of hand. I probably saw them once. There would be a roomful of drunken Cleveland State students; the show would [climax] with bottles being thrown and equipment being broken and fistfights in the audience. It was chaotic and they were doing it as performance art, trying to evoke a reaction.
>
> At that time Devo started playing around here, Pere Ubu started doing their thing, and there were a lot of new-wave bands coming up from Akron . . . Hammer Damage and Chi-Pig. Chi-Pig were so cool; they'd come on stage, girls in white shirts and black ties, and again it was just part of that whole new wave movement. Hammer Damage, just good rock and roll.
>
> It was really a nurturing time and you definitely wanted to be a part of it. Get three or four friends together, start a band, there'd be venues to play.
>
> **—Tom Lash, musician (Lucky Pierre and Hot Tin Roof)**

A WORKING ALTERNATIVE BAND:

For a few years in the early '80s, Lucky Pierre worked nearly every night of the week. The Lakewood band was one of the few alternative groups to do that.

IF YOU MISSED OUT ON HIGH SCHOOL—here's a second chan
HERE'S HOW YOU CAN ATTRACT A LOVER NOW!
FOR MEN!
FOR WOMEN!
July 26
PIRATE'S COVE
Wild Giraffes
-w-
Hammer Damage

The Generators were Glenn Toszer ("Stutz Bearcat"), Don Buchanan, Frank Musarra, Cathy Dottore ("Eva Dilcue"), and Mark Addison. A spin-off of Buzzy Linhart's band, they formed in 1979 and played places like Peabody's Café in Cleveland Heights and the Flipside, near the old Mayfield Theater.

> We had been breaking out from Buzzy and doing our own material; we called ourselves the Buzzards, like the MMS Buzzards. So we played solo one Friday night, left the gig, got into the van, drove to New York City, and played two radio shows, live on the air with Buzzy. Drove right back to Cleveland, actually to Oberlin, to play again as the Buzzards, outdoors, it was

October, 34 degrees. The goofiness was we were becoming our own band, and there was some trouble, mostly between Buzzy and Mark Addison, it was just getting messy. We played a second Coffee Break Concert, and now they were live at Bobby McGee's, across from the Palace. So we're playing all Buzzy songs, we're just about through, and Buzzy said, "I feel very bad announcing this, but this is the very last show we're going to be playing together as a band." He basically fired us on the air. We had some more songs to do. It was just weird; he turns around, he comes to me, "You're going to stay with me, right?" I said, "Buzzy, we have to talk about this."

I played some dates with him here and there, but we were still the Buzzards. We recorded "TV Set" as a demo and sent it to the MMS Record Deal contest, and we won. Then we played another Coffee Break Concert with Len Goldberg, and on the air, we changed our name to the Heaters, Len was the first to announce it. I think the next day we got a cease and desist order from a band in California; so then we became the Generators. At that point, I was already planning on leaving. —**Frank Musarra, musician (the Generators)**

"He basically fired us on the air. We had some more songs to do. It was just weird."

I had been playing with Buzzy Linhart, and I was very headstrong and, I'm sure, did something to offend him. He came up to me and said, "Addison, fuck you, the band's yours," and that turned into the Generators. We entered some kind of MMS contest, and we won. We got a free session at Agency Recording; then we put a single out, I think, we were on the Buzzard something label, but by that point it had become a farce, the whole Buzzard thing—the Best of Cleveland or whatever it was, Pride of Cleveland, that's what it was. Mostly really trash, junky corporate bands. I was part of that.

I think Cleveland was a really provincial city and there was never anybody who had any kind of realistic viewpoint on how the music business actually worked. I certainly took everything the wrong way and certainly didn't have anyone to tell me any differently. —**Mark Addison, musician (the Generators, A Nation of One)**

The Generators push showed the hypocrisy of MMS breaking bands as long as they were on a major label; there was another band that John Gorman was going to break, American Noise. His claim was if we can break these guys, we can break anybody. And labels will have to do what we say. He backed the wrong horse. —**Tom Lash, musician**

A BAND THAT NEVER QUITS:

Wild Horses has been playing straight rock and roll for decades, scoring a 1980 hit with "Funky Poodle."

My Favorite Northeast Ohio Bands

by Peanuts, *longtime Cleveland music journalist*

1. The Raspberries
2. The Dazz Band
3. Michael Stanley Band
4. I Don't Care
5. Forecast
6. Robert Lockwood Jr.'s band
7. The Generators
8. Rastus
9. American Noise
10. Circus

Dewey Forward, who used to own Peabody's Down Under, the hottest Flats club in the '80s and '90s, had high hopes for A Nation of One, the band Addison formed after the Generators broke up. Seven record labels sniffed around but none bit.

> They said we had a great musician on our hands but it was the advent of MTV, videos, pretty boys. We brought in a guy from L.A. to choreograph them who blocked them and gave them moves, made them more MTV-available. It looked ridiculous on Mark and the band. They dressed him up like Bruce Springsteen, gave him a mousse hairdo, gave him spots on the stage to hit, and poses. This was after the first few record labels had passed on him because he was not video-ready. Here we're trying to patch it up, we got three more record labels coming to town. It was embarrassing. Here's Mark, he's trying to do this, it's so unnatural, so it never happened. All seven turned them down, same reasons, wasn't charismatic enough on stage, even though his music was just superb, maybe the best stuff that ever came out of Cleveland. —**Dewey Forward, former club owner**

God knows, the Numbers Band has always played bars. But originality sets it several cuts above, not to mention perseverance. Other bands play cover material and become known for their stand at a bar, like Mr. Stress at the Euclid Tavern; and others, like a band that impressed David Bowie at Hennessy's, have a brush with fame—once.

Bill Miller is Mr. Stress. He's been working for forty years, and everybody from mainstreamers like the James Gang's Jimmy Fox to undergrounders like Anton Fier, drummer for Ubu and the Golden Palominos, has passed through his group. Chrissie Hynde worked in Stress, briefly; Peter Laughner apprenticed there. Stress can remember when folk turned to rock. The place was La Cave:

> The first jobs we had were July of 1967, I think the 12th and 13th, it was a Tuesday and Wednesday, they gave us as a local act. They had been doing acoustic and folk, and had not done electric to any great degree at that point. That lineup had Glenn Schwartz on guitar; he was gigging with me if Jimmy [Fox] didn't have work for him. Glenn was a blues musician at that time, head and shoulders above everybody else. The first time we played there, they thought we were the loudest thing they'd ever heard. Glenn was never a shrinking violet. Within a month or two, they started bringing in the Velvet Underground, the Fugs—and all of a sudden we weren't too loud anymore.
>
> Between '68 and about '71, I did a lot of work in ghetto bars like Jiffy's, on East 71st and Lexington, by League Park; it went up in the riots in '71 and got destroyed. Another place was Joe D's Cozy Room at East 133rd and

HOOKING UP WITH THE BUZZARD:

The Generators looked like the next big thing when the Buzzard gave the band its blessing by way of a record deal. But the buzz never made it out of Cleveland.

My Favorite Northeast Ohio Bands and Musicians

by Tom Feran, *Cleveland Plain Dealer columnist*

- Pere Ubu
- Beau Coup
- Joey and the Continentals
- The Twilighters (Steve Popovich's band)
- The Hesitations
- Arthur Alexander
- Johnny Cymbal ("Mr. Bass Man")
- Derek ("Cinnamon")
- Screamin' Jay Hawkins

Northeast Ohio Bands and Performers Who Made Their Mark in the 1970s

Alex Bevan
American Noise
Atlantis Philharmonic
Backdoor Men
Bardot
John Bassette
Bell Telephunk
Bernie and the Invisibles
Bizarros
Bock
Bomber's Moon
Buckeye Biscuit
The Case of E.T. Hooley
Charade
Chi-Pig
Cinderella Backstreet
Circus
Climax
Cottonmouth
Dazz Band
Dead Boys
Deadly Earnest
Devo
Dragonwyck (originally the Morticians)
Dust

Miles; we worked under the name Swamp Fever, because I didn't want the union knowing I was scabbing in some other clubs. You wanted to work, just like these guys do today working in two or three bands.

We would have sometimes a black bass player named Ernest Goode, I know he's gone, and a various and sundry collection of black drummers who you'd meet for one night and never see again. I took pride in playing for black people who were forty-five to sixty years old, who knew what I was trying to do and liked it. They respected it, they enjoyed it, they danced to it, they partied to it. I've never had complaints from black audiences about being white and playing black music.

We had developed a following of young white kids. Bob Frank, the leader of Blue Lunch, started bringing these high school girls with him, and the fellows in the bar would ask them to dance and the kids would get bent out of shape. One night one of the customers started coming after me. It was a brawl. You figure the short, fat guy looks easy. I picked up a mike stand and hit him over the back of his shoulder blade area; he had a hard time getting up again. People will tell you stories about me chasing people out of the Euclid Tavern with a gun. Even now I have to watch myself; my pride is so close to the surface that I react. —**Bill Miller, musician (Mr. Stress Blues Band)**

"They thought we were the loudest thing they'd ever heard. Within a month or two, they started bringing in the Velvet Underground, the Fugs—and all of a sudden we weren't too loud anymore."

THE BLUES LABORATORY: **Bill "Mr. Stress" Miller (he's the guy at the center of this mid-'80s version of the Mr. Stress Blues Band) has been working area bars since the '60s. Like the Numbers Band, Mr. Stress keeps on keeping on.**

The atmosphere wasn't quite so volatile when David Bowie dropped into Hennessy's:

Once upon a time I was managing a band called Labrynth. They were playing at Hennessy's, now the Hi-Fi Club, 11729 Detroit Avenue, Lakewood. It was 1972 or 1973, whenever Bowie played Music Hall. The place wasn't all that crowded because a lot of people had gone to see Bowie. Bowie gets done with the show, he loads the limo up, he goes to the Cleveland Agora, which at that point was at the East 24th Street location. Even then the Agora was known as the place to go because of their concerts, the Monday night concert series. What Bowie didn't know was that [this was a Saturday-night crowd]. All the college jocks see Bowie and are making fun of him, like hey, who's the faggot with the orange hair? Bowie goes back to the limo driver says, forget this, where else can we go?

It was American Ambulance Limousine in Lakewood, which is right next to Hennessy's. The ambulance driver says we have a place in Lakewood that plays music; Bowie says let's go. It's 1 in the morning. The late Leo Cronin is standing at the front door, he'd dropped acid earlier in the evening, all of a sudden this black guy in a suit comes in. In the early '70s, you don't have a lot of black guys in suits coming into Lakewood. It's Bowie's bodyguard, he's from Jamaica, and the guy goes, "I say, by Jove, can we bring David Bowie in the place?"

Leo says, "Sure, buddy, whoever the guy is."

The bodyguard leaves. Leo yells over at the owner—his nickname was Father Fred Mills—"Hey, David Bowie's going to show up." Fred knows Leo's high, knows he's cooked.

But about a minute later, a limo shows up in front. It's like a Chinese fire drill where all the doors open. It's all the disc jockeys from WGCL, what WNCX used to be. The last guy out of the limo is this guy with orange hair, green jumpsuit with a cape, and it's Bowie. Leo gets like a pinball machine; he's got a head full of acid, Bowie just walked in. I'm standing in the back, Father Fred looks up to me and goes, "David Bowie's here."

I said, "Get out."

Fred goes, "Leo just told me."

I said, "Fred, Leo's tripping." At that point, I walk by the table and say, "Leo, is David Bowie here?" Leo's talking some kind of Portuguese, he's gone. So now I start walking back, I get about halfway back, I see Bowie at a table, I say, Oh my God, Leo's right.

I'm trying to get the band alert to this—they're in the middle of a set—however the rhythm guitarist has already seen what happened, he turns to the rest of the band like the idiot he is, says, let's do the Bowie medley. They

Eastwind
Electric Eels
Eli Radish
Euclid Beach Band
Euphrates
Fayrewether
Featherstitch
First Light
Flatbush
Friction
Gangreen
Gay Marshal and the Basin Street Elite
Granicus
Hessler Court
Hieronymus Bosch
Human Switchboard
James Gang
Jewel Of The Deep
Kinsman Dazz
Don Kriss & the Vettes
Labrynth
Lepers
Little Willie and the All Stars
Magic
Maxx Band
The Mirrors
Mushroom
Natchez Trace
Pere Ubu
Poe
Rainbow Canyon
The Raspberries
Rastus
Reign
Rocket from the Tombs
Rubber City Rebels
Shelter
Skezix
Snow
Mr. Stress
Strutter

Styrene Money Band
Rachel Sweet
Sweetleaf
Target
Tin Huey
Tiny Alice
Tootz
Wild Butter
Wild Horses
Willio and Phillio
X Blank X

Northeast Ohio Bands and Performers That Made Their Mark in the 1980s

Adults
Beau Coup
Breathless
Call Off Your Dog
A Cellarful of Noise
The Clocks
Death of Samantha
Exotic Birds
The Generators
The Innocent
Legendary Pink Holes
LeVert
Love Affair
Lucky Pierre
My Dad Is Dead
A Nation of One
New Salem Witch Hunters
Nine Inch Nails
Michael Stanley Band
Pony Boys
Prisonshake
Slam Bamboo
Mr. Stress
Waitresses
Wild Giraffes

go right into it, they did it, a three-song Bowie medley. I'm going, okay, so they did a Bowie medley. Then Jim McCarthy, the singer, says let's do the Jethro Tull medley. So they start with "Aqualung," he gets to the lead, all of a sudden, I see Bowie stop talking, he's looking around, trying to figure out who's doing the lead—it's Carl Wesley, the lead guitar, on the other side of the stage. At this point, Bowie gets up, walks over to the back room where the johns are and sits down, and that's when the band realizes it is Bowie and they'd just done a Bowie medley.

Bowie set up a round of drinks for the band. I guess he liked the Jethro Tull medley. —**Peanuts, former band manager**

"The last guy out of the limo is this guy with orange hair, green jumpsuit with a cape, and it's Bowie."

Years after Dragonwyck broke up, drummer Dale Flanigan found himself playing with Jimmy Landers, a veteran of the Leo's Casino house band, in a different kind of club:

It was at Sailor's Bar in Eastlake in 1989, '90, '91. I come in and unload my drums, I'm the first one there, Jimmy Hoare, plays with Lockwood now, tossed me this job, calls them cabaret jobs—cabaret jobs generally meant an after-hours place that didn't have a liquor license. The guys that went there, their personal profile was they were probably Hell's Angels who got drafted so they came back and became hit men or beer truck or cement truck drivers or a combination thereof. There was this guy with no neck working the door. He said, "Why don't you bring your drums in the side door, I'll give you a hand."

I said, "Cool."

He asked, "What kind of music you guys play?"

And in the door comes Jimmy Landers, the leader.

The doorman turned to me and said, "Are there niggers in this band?"

I said, "Actually, I'm just filling in, I'm the only white guy."

He said to me, "Are you kidding?"

I said no.

He said, "See this door? I'm going to be guarding this door next to the stage, and if some shit goes down, you come out this door, but I can't guarantee anything else."

As each band member came in and started setting their gear up, it got quieter and quieter. Everybody in the place, it was like a time warp, man.

They were all wearing rebel T-shirts. There was a guy looked like Big Daddy Roth, the car customizer, he had a tattooed face and neck and he was kind of the head guy—nobody you'd even like to make face contact with, the guy was so fucking frightening. And everybody starts loading in, it's getting quieter and quieter and weirder and weirder, and the guitar player, they called him Doc something, he had this huge 'fro stuffed into a baseball cap, he brought his amp in and his guitar and went over to Landers, said, "What's happening?" Landers said there might be an issue of some kind; it might be a misbooking.

Doc walks over to the bar. The bartender comes over to him, Doc says, "Which one of you white motherfuckers wants to buy me a drink?" It was dead silent for like three eternal seconds, and the big guy who looked like Daddy Roth said, "I'll buy that nigger a drink." It broke the ice. It was the best job we ever had. We laid the funk on them, the blues funk on them. They were asking for hillbilly tunes, it was fantastic. He was either going to buy him a drink or blow his head off. —**Dale Flanigan, musician (Dragonwyck)**

Agora favorite Todd Rundgren blasts off at his favorite club.

HANGOUTS & HOTSPOTS

Clubs

Before rock went corporate, armories in downtown Cleveland, Akron, Chagrin, and Painesville presented local acts. So did Hullabaloos, especially those in Mentor, Chesterland, and North Ridgeville. Kids could groove to the hottest local groups of the day like the James Gang, the Mods and the Choir, Glass Harp—and imports like the Yardbirds, Terry Knight and the Pack, and the Stooges.

We used to see the Mods at Chagrin Armory a lot, even before they were the Choir. They'd do their set and then pick the cutest girls to make out with on their breaks. I remember Dave Burke, we always thought he was really, really cool. He had this long hair, and he had gotten in trouble for something, and he had to go to court and they made him cut his hair. I remember he came to a gig and he had this dorky, short haircut. He was like a skinny little boy. We were all shocked at how uncool he was without his hair. He was feeling really uncool, too. I remember him hanging at the side.
—Sue Vendetti, fan (Brunswick)

There were lots of high school dances, sock hops they called them, in the gyms. There was a big buzz around the Mods. I can remember one time they came to play at the Chagrin Armory; they were late from playing somewhere else, and they had a manager named Ray Taylor who drove an old, big black Lincoln. He limoed them around, so when they get there, Ray comes in saying, make way for the Mods, make way for the Mods. The place was packed. The teen clubs were always highly chaperoned, kind of like parents looking down their nose at you, and the sock hops, you had teachers everywhere.

There wasn't really anywhere to be a kid, but these armories did that. Whoever rented them out knew kids needed a place where the lights could be low and it could be kind of a . . . it was our version of the Cavern [where the Beatles perfected their craft in Liverpool]. It was sort of a big, open, dark place, grungy place, and it created a really fun atmosphere. They were cool.

Cleveland's Notable Rock and Roll Venues of the 1960s

Agora (E. 24th St.)
Berea Armory
Brunswick Hullabaloo, Laurel Square Shopping Center
Cat's Meow (High St. downtown)
Chagrin Armory
The Cell, Lakewood (in the basement of City Hall)
Chippewa Lake Park
Cleveland Arena
Cyrus Erie West (formerly the North Ridgeville Hullabaloo)
The Dove
D'Poo's Tool and Dye Works
The English Grille (University Circle)
Euclid Beach Park
Euphoria, E. 15th and Euclid Ave. (became Alice's Restaurant)
Fairview Park Legion Hall, Lorain Rd.
Geauga Lake
Gleason's Musical Bar
Grande Ballroom (now WHK Auditorium/the Agora)
Green Darby 140th and Lakeshore
Hire's Lounge, Euclid Ave., Wickliffe (originally Johnny's Lounge)
Jazz Temple, University Circle
Jicky's After Dark
Joe D's Cozy Room, E. 133rd and Miles Rd.

Cleveland's Notable Rock and Roll Venues of the 1960s cont'd.

La Cave
Leo's Cafe, E. 75th and St. Clair Ave.
Leo's Casino, E. 75th and Euclid Ave.
The Library (Prospect Ave.)
Lorain Hullabaloo, Kamm's Corners
Luccioni's, Richmond Hts.
Mentor Hullabaloo
Municipal Stadium
Musicarnival
Otto's Grotto in the Statler Hilton
Painesville Armory
Park Lane (16800 Brookpark Rd.)
Parkview Legion Hall, Fairview Park
Playboy Lounge (16800 Lorain Rd.)
The Pinwheel
The Plato
St. John's Hall
The Sands, Portage Lakes
Shibley's Sahara Lounge, Willoughby Hills
Silver Dollar, W. 110th and Lorain
Tap Room, Parma (later the Band Box)
Teen Town, Mayfield Rd., S. Euclid
The Torchlight, Mentor
The Virginian, Shaker Hts.
Tramend Lounge, E. 55th and Broadway Ave.
Yankee Bar, Detroit Ave. (later the Happy Dog)

The armories really were fun places to go, and they often would do multiple band things. Those went—from probably '66—at least two, three years. By the time the Hullabaloos were going strong, I don't think people were going to the armories anymore. The armories were before there were any other real clubs where kids could go. There were bars, but not clubs.
—Ken Margolis, musician (Rebel Kind, the Choir)

When we were in high school they used to have dances at the armory in Painesville, and there was one in Chagrin. The one band I used to go see with my friends was called Kicks, Inc. I remember Terry Knight came to play there; I'm pretty sure [Bob] Seger might have played one, too. I remember seeing Seger in Columbus at the time "Heavy Music" was out. It was inside of an armory. They had this one big, open room. They were fun to go to, this was a big social thing. The other thing is they would bring in bands that had a hit record or two; it was another nice place you could see that.
—Don Sebian, fan (Cleveland Heights)

The Hullabaloos were the link between the armories and the Agora and flourished before rock went big-time:

I played bass with the Dead Boys. I grew up in Mentor, Ohio, and the Mentor Hullabaloo nightspot was my entire rock world in the early '70s. Across from the Great Lakes Mall, this place must have had a dozen different names before becoming Hullabaloo or Rock Shop. I have a distant memory of it as the Torchlight, and people like Billy J. Kramer and Terry Knight would play there. It was walking distance from where I lived. I remember seeing Alice Cooper there, when *Love It to Death* came out, for two dollars, and they were fucking brilliant. The James Gang came back from their first English tour opening for the Who and the place was S.R.O. I was broke and club owner Otto Neuber finally let me in just to shut me up.

The James Gang had all these Hiwatt amplifiers with "The Who" stenciled on the back, and they were playing their old songs *Live at Leeds* style—long, drawn-out versions, with lots of improvisation. Glenn Schwartz would come in there with his trio and just burn a hole in that stage. He was great. Other dusty memories: Captain Foam and the Doctor (a guitar player and a drummer with a huge double drum set—the songs were just jams), Bob Seger System, Brownsville Station, Frut (with their fab backup singers, the Famed Warblers!), Damnation of Adam Blessing. I saw the Stooges there and, in between songs, Iggy read off a list of license plate numbers of cars in the parking lot with their headlights left on!

"The Mentor Hullabaloo nightspot was my entire rock world in the early '70s."

One local band named Poe comes to mind. They had a killer guitar player named Ralph Kuta. He was something else. I spent alotta nights in that club and, when the bands sucked, you'd slurp Cokes, smoke cigarettes, and play the Gottlieb "Four Seasons" pinball machine in the back. —**Jeff Magnum, musician (Dead Boys)**

My favorite was Mentor Hullabaloo. My favorite local bands there were Cyrus Erie, Target, Poe, Moses, E.T. Hooley, Eli Radish, Freeport Express. I went there from '67—I believe, it closed around '70 or '71 at the latest. Basically, it started out as a club just for kids thirteen to eighteen or nineteen, but it kind of evolved. I'm guessing it probably held about 350, maybe 400 tops. People have said 1,000, and there's no way the place held 1,000.

I never could see how the place ever made any money. It was generally open only on Friday and Saturday night; sometimes they'd have a show on a Wednesday if school was out. I think the regular admission was $1.50. National bands? Alice Cooper, the Amboy Dukes; they had a lot of the Detroit bands—Bob Seger, SRC. I remember seeing Terry Knight and the Pack at the Painesville Armory, I don't remember seeing them at the Mentor Hullabaloo. Alice Cooper was, well, everybody in the band had the longest hair that anybody had seen by then, that was the thing that stood out for me. I don't even think *Easy Action* had come out yet. They played Mentor Hullabaloo, I believe at least twice, and they played J.B.'s at Kent, also. I always had a car; I had my father's station wagon. —**Brad Bell, fan (Chagrin Falls)**

This dates to 1967 or 1968, from a former dancer in Brunswick:

We would dance onstage in front of the bands. There were two of us. We didn't have a cage, though, and didn't have to wear white boots like they did on the TV show. It was always for a live band, and the biggest band was the Choir. I actually made the owner of the club buy this psychedelic, tie-dyed material, and I made us culotte dresses. Under black light, they would go all swirly. It was eighteen and under, and the owner's wife picked out the pattern and I could sew. They were culottes, so when you were onstage, nobody could look up your skirt, but they were short.

Ironically, for being such a small town, we had three different dance clubs: the Hullabaloo, the Sound Project, and every Friday night for years

STRICTLY FOR TEENS: Betcha some groovy little notes were written on pads like this Hullabaloo Scene keepsake.

THE REAL THING: Turn in one of these, and you'd get a Coke. Probably not a Big Gulp.

there were teen dances with live music at the Civic Room over the bowling alley. And Brunswick Lakes, which is now a Giant Eagle, used to have a pavilion, with a teen dance on Saturday nights. And then Chippewa Lake, in their pavilion, used to do battles of the bands at least once a month. Cyrus Erie were big back then. It amazes me that somehow it all died off. Live music is better than canned—always. The KYW DJ who was very big, Jerry G, my dad said he sounded just like Donald Duck. We thought he was great. We used to get the list. We'd walk to Woolworth's; Woolworth's in Laurel Square always had the list every Friday. —**Lyn Byrd, fan (Cleveland)**

The Agora Legend

The Agora is still going strong at 55th and Euclid, but a fire in 1984 snuffed out its most famous address, 1730 E. 24th Street. Every rock body who was anybody played there between the late '60s and mid-'80s. It was a franchise; at its peak, founder Hank LoConti operated thirteen Agoras in ten cities. It's where Bruce Springsteen performed one of his most famous concerts. It's where Plasmatics bimbo Wendy O. Williams scandalized Jane Scott in 1981. It's where WMMS staged its Coffee Break Concerts and where the best roadies in the business trained. If there's a Mount Rushmore of Cleveland rock clubs, the Agora is the most prominent carving.

My favorite club was and still is the Agora, in its various forms. When I was a kid, it seemed that just about every rock group had the potential for superstardom, and when LoConti would present acts like Argent, Bob Seger, T. Rex, National Lampoon's "Lemmings" (with John Belushi), or even Lenny and the Squigtones it was always an event. —**Mike Olszewski, fan (Aurora)**

The first Agora opened on Cornell Road near Case Western Reserve University in 1966. A year later it moved to this location on East 24th Street (seen here on August 9, 1967), where Cleveland State students came to watch local groups.

I almost always was at the Monday Nights Out at the Agora, the "101 shows" that would become the "202 shows." First it was a $1.01 concert, then it became a $2.02 concert. You'd catch everybody who was coming out on their first album. A lot of musicians would go there and hang out; most Monday and Tuesday nights were concert nights. Monday night would be MMS concerts; they'd sponsor Tuesday nights, too, but sometimes those would be just straight, regular concerts. It was almost always packed—that's anywhere between 1975 and 1982. I'd call that one of

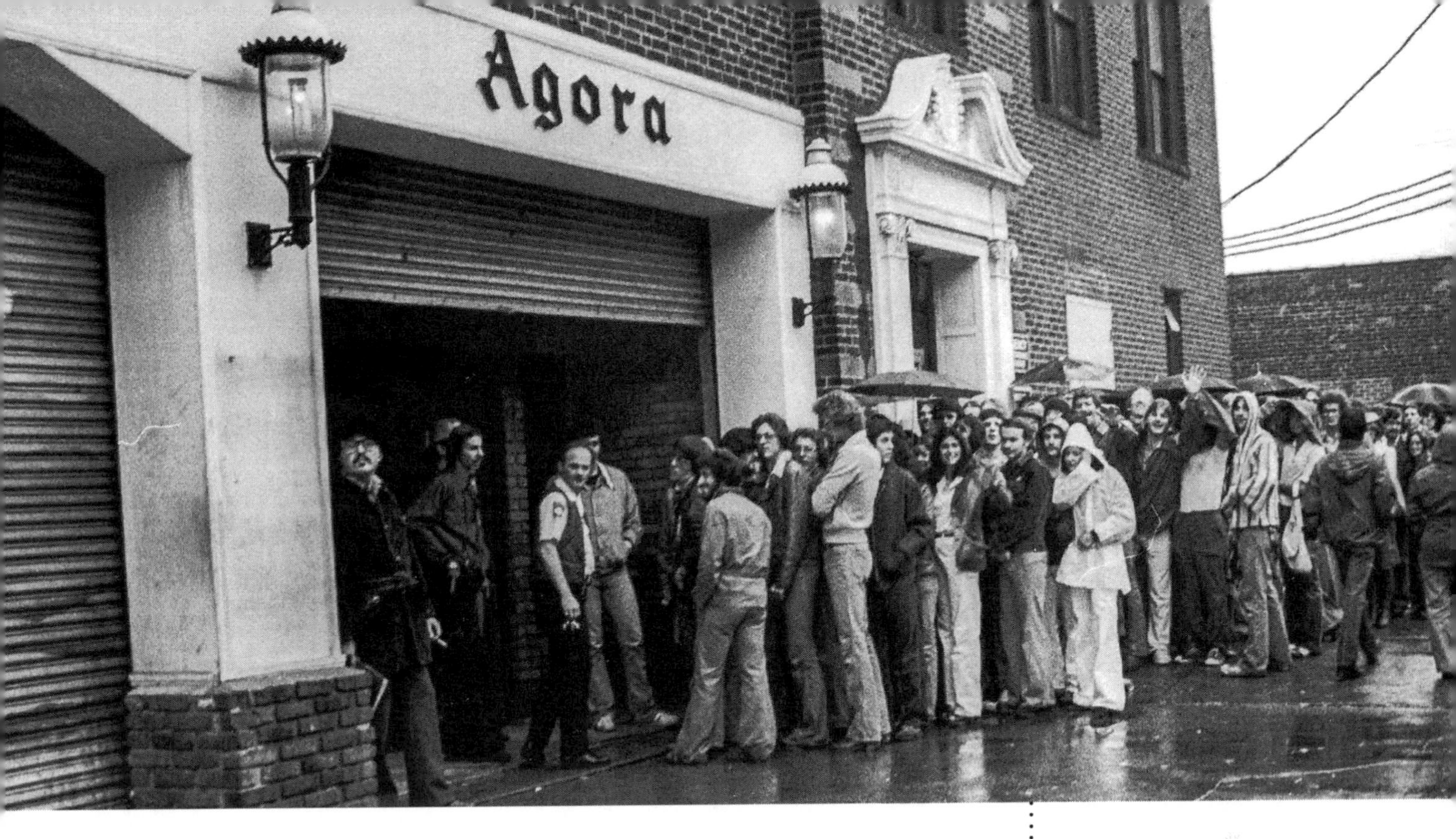

the big tragedies of Cleveland when the Agora was moved to where they have it now. That was a Cleveland rock and roll landmark. Young people couldn't wait until they were old enough to go there.

We started playing the Cleveland Agora on Thursday nights right after Circus folded. I believe it was '75, the Cleveland Agora was like the shining jewel. I remember one time saying all I wanted to do was play the Cleveland Agora; it was a big deal at the time to be playing there and be so young—I'm standing onstage where all my heroes played. —**Rich Spina, musician (Love Affair)**

"I remember one time saying all I wanted to do was play the Cleveland Agora."

There's a piece of the stage from the old Agora in the new one. That's where Bruce Springsteen stood when he did the anniversary concert, that's where everybody that was anybody stood. It was like holy ground. —**Carole Singleton-Chase, fan (North Olmsted)**

We had a farm system, and it was especially good here because it was Hank, having the Agora and really not wanting to get into the concert field. He would lay the first foundation, and we would take it from there and take that artist into a Music Hall and then into a Public Hall and then into the

HAVING A PARTY:
Wet and cold didn't keep a line from forming for a Southside Johnny and the Asbury Jukes show at the Agora on May 2, 1977.

HANK'S PLACE:

That's Hank LoConti, owner, at the top, his head obscuring part of the Agora Ballroom sign. Buddy Maver, his manager, is fourth from left, in suspenders, on the bottom row.

stadium. If Hank had been more ambitious to the extent he really wanted to get into the concert business, it could have been Hank doing those concerts. In those days there was a loyalty in that the first person doing something would get the next crack, kind of a loyalty system. —**Jules Belkin, promoter**

King of Cleveland

Marc Cohn wangled himself onto a Coffee Break Concert in the mid-'70s, when he was still a student at Beachwood High School.

The show was sort of the original *Unplugged,* right? Recording artists would come through town, drop by, and play. I'd started writing from the time I was twelve, thirteen, fourteen, I loved hearing the way a song sounded in the only context I knew, which was just me playing with a guitar. The first songs I ever wrote were all on guitar; I didn't really start playing piano until I was about nineteen. So I was a huge fan of MMS and a huge fan of that show, so I kept bugging the program director to try to convince him to get me on the show. The only people who were on that show as far as I knew were signed recording artists. I wasn't a recording artist yet, and I certainly wasn't signed. But at some point he succumbed, I don't remember why. I finally got through, they got me on MMS, it was not only a huge thing for me but for all my friends listening in from school.

It's an embarrassing relic to me now, but it was a huge, huge event to me back then. It can be bootlegged somehow—I played the full hour, I was completely unknown, just this local Cleveland kid they let take the airwaves for an hour. I was seventeen, I didn't get signed until I was twenty-eight. When I have heard on various websites samples of what it sounds like, it's like a sonic version of looking at your high school picture. You can't even recognize who it is anymore.

IN THE MOVIES:

Paul Simon spent six weeks at the Agora filming his movie *One Trick Pony* in 1979.

I was extremely nervous; you can hear that, too. At the time I sounded like a lot of the people that influenced me back then; I hadn't found my voice at all as a songwriter or a singer. So on one song I sound like Cat Stevens, on another song I sound like James Taylor. It's sort of a big mess. But I had a lot of nerve and I guess I had a lot of stick-to-it-iveness because somehow I got on that show. And I really didn't belong there yet. But at the time I thought I was king of Cleveland. —**Marc Cohn, musician (winner, Grammy Award for Best New Artist of 1991 for "Walking in Memphis")**

IN PERFECT HARMONY:

WMMS and the Agora made beautiful music (and business) together.

The Coffee Break Concerts were made available because groups were coming into town to do concerts at night and MMS saw an opportunity to promote the band and themselves. It could have been Kid Leo and Matt the Cat who would introduce these bands. They would take place at twelve o'clock to one, a part of the day where you would not normally hear a band anywhere in the country at that time. They were at the Agora. The Agora was a pretty big space and the bar was open at noon.

This was kind of like the hipster's version of the three-martini lunch. I would meet my friends there. I was working with Sun Newspapers at the time, maybe out in North Olmsted, so I don't know how I managed to get myself downtown for those things. We would meet with a whole bunch of other people. There were a lot of wild chicks. It was almost like a Browns crowd, that working-class-hero crowd who would go to these events. We would have plenty to drink. I remember one of my friends saying to me, any girl who stays past 1:30, you know she was loose, she's not going back to work. I also remember smoking weed in there; there were a lot of people smoking weed in there. It was much more lax back then.

"It was almost like a Browns crowd, that working-class-hero crowd who would go to these events."

As far as who we saw there, one of the first I remember was Boxcar Willie. But that's a perfect example of what these things were about: it wasn't so much who was playing, it was being downtown and an excuse to get a little wild. I saw Wendy O. Williams; there were probably a lot of local guys like Michael Stanley and such. It was a live radio broadcast, so if you couldn't go to it, you could always tune it in. But after it was over, we would stay and still have drinks, and drinks were really dirt cheap back then.

September 2, 1975

Mr. Hank LoConti
The Agora Club
1730 East 24th St.
Cleveland, Ohio 44114

Dear Hank:

It was a pleasure working with you, as the advertising vehicle for your recent outdoor concert. We were proud to be part of the excitement, and we look forward to another similar event in the future to add to the high impact "Monday Nights Out at The Agora".

We work well together, let's continue that succe[illegible]d next year, we won't let it rain either!

Best regards,

Walt A. Tiburski, Jr.
Local Sales Manager, WMMS

P.S. People from all over were interested, [illegible]

dak

Enclosure

5000 Euclid Avenue, Cleveland,

Kid Leo

LOAFIN' AROUND:

Meat Loaf and crew backstage at the Agora after the 1978 Cleveland International Showcase. That's Ian Hunter on the far right, the songwriter who penned "Cleveland Rocks."

The concerts were free. They wanted to fill the place because they wanted it to sound impressive when they did the broadcast. There would be hundreds of people there—even for Boxcar Willie, the place was packed. And on occasion, a fight would break out. It was just a crazy throwback you wouldn't see anymore. Back then, when I was twenty-four or twenty-five years old, it was really the essence of Cleveland's rock and roll spirit. It was sex, drugs, and rock and roll basically. It's so unreal today that something like that would take place downtown. It was acceptable for you to have three martinis at lunch. —**Mike Sanson, fan (Lakewood)**

Before the Agora there were two other legendary clubs: Leo's Casino and La Cave de Café, or La Cave. Leo's was at 7500 Euclid, La Cave at 10165 Euclid. Where Leo's will forever be associated with Motown, La Cave is where folk turned into rock and roll.

I was a student at Cleveland Heights High School, and like a lot of other Jewish boys growing up in the suburbs of big cities, I loved soul music and rhythm and blues. So I wanted to go to Leo's, I had heard about the place, and a friend told me it was okay for white people to go there, you just had to duke the doorman $5. For me, $5 was a lot of money. By the way, the $5 didn't count toward the cover charge or the drink minimum. So this was going to be an expensive night for me, but Sam & Dave were coming, and they were double dynamite, so I was hot to see them. So I invited my girlfriend and I said we're going to have a night out. And she liked the music, too, and she liked to dance. She always said I was the best dancer she'd ever gone out with.

So very nervously, we went down to Leo's Casino. I borrowed my father's '58 Chevy, and I got to tell you, I was scared. I just didn't know what to expect. I had never gone into a "black" club before, I didn't have a clue. But we went, and I duked the doorman $5, and it was no problem whatsoever. It's a nightclub setting, small tables, chairs around them. Yes, we got looks, but everybody was cool, and we sang along, and we had a great night. Of course, I didn't get laid. But it wasn't about getting laid, it was about having a great time. And it was amazing that we were treated well.

So here's my girlfriend's story; I dated her all through college and all through high school. Her name is Laurie Wieder. Her memory of the date is that she was pretty nervous, too, and although no one hassled us and it was cool, she realized very quickly she was dressed wrong. When I told her we were going to a concert, she dressed like she was going to Severance Hall, the only kind of concert she knew how to dress for. No one hassled her, no one commented on it. We get home from the date, I drop her off, her father was up waiting for her, and he says, did you have a good time, where did you go? She tells her father she went to Leo's Casino. He wagged his finger in her face and said, I can't believe you went there, don't you ever go there again, and who is that boy who would take you there, I don't want you ever to see him again. Obviously, his admonition did no good.

In a way, her ending makes the story. I'm more proud of our chutzpah in doing it—we felt we were taking a risk—but in fact there was no reason to be afraid. —**Howard Landau, fan (Shaker Heights)**

"She tells her father she went to Leo's Casino. He wagged his finger in her face and said, don't you ever go there again."

Four years later, there was. The occasion was a Supremes show in July 1966, the time of the Hough riots.

That was during the time of the civil rights movement, and it wasn't the greatest time for African-Americans and one of the most significant contributions of rock and roll is it probably single-handedly in many instances

A GOOD TIME? YOU BET: Maybe you couldn't gamble at Leo's Casino, but some of the hottest acts to pass through Cleveland played this stage, including Otis Redding—in his final performance.

brought the races together: This one night, in the midst of the Hough riots, when National Guard tanks were rolling down the streets of Euclid Avenue, you had white people coming down to 75th and Euclid to Leo's Casino to see the Supremes. Leo's was what many people would call a club on the chitlin' circuit and a hub for Berry Gordy's artists coming down from Detroit to perform, and even before then they would have these wonderful artists performing these three shows on the weekend. I think they may have even started Thursday night. These same people would more often than not be on the *Upbeat* show on Saturday afternoon. Not only the Motown people but R&B people in general.

The atmosphere that night was extremely tense. The people were so enamored and excited about the Supremes they failed to understand the gravity of the situation. The National Guard got on the stage and said, you people have to go home. It seems that was the recognition, when it hit people how tense the situation really was.

The Supremes were scared to death and they suspended the show.
—Ruthie Brown, fan (Shaker Heights)

"The Supremes were scared to death and they suspended the show."

It was the night Otis Redding performed his last show, at Leo's December 9, 1967:

It was something else. Otis Redding had a style of his own, and the band was so tight. It was just devastating. He'd sweat up; he was a hard performer. Also, Jackie Wilson, he was a hard performer. His thing was as he performed, he would lie down on the corner of the stage and all the ladies would line up and everybody would come by and kiss him on the mouth. They'd line up. **—Chris Wright, fan (Cleveland)**

At Leo's Casino there were some great moments, because that happened during a period when the O'Jays not successful recording artists, we were basically regional recording artists. We were good in Detroit, Pittsburgh, Akron, we might go to Chicago, we might go to North Carolina. We were in Cleveland because we stayed there, this would have to be about 1967; did a date with the Temptations. It was one of the probably most talked about dates in ours and the Temptations' career. It was six nights of R&B singing groups, doo-wop, the best you could ever get. The people were there every night, in line, standing outside, begging to get in; we did two shows a night,

My Favorite Shows at the REAL Agora (1730 E. 24th St.)

by Buddy Maver

Agora Manager (who booked all of these except #10 and #6)

10. ZZ Top: They played a last-set show for free on a Friday night (dance night) in 1969 after my group, Charade, finished. They were completely unknown outside of Texas. The place cleared out quickly, but I stayed and saw an incredible show by the then-beardless trio.

9. Sex Pistols: Actually, a non-show. There was tremendous hype about their first tour of America. The Agora was the favorite place for all the British bands, and their agent wanted the Agora to be the first date on the tour. I booked them, the show sold out, and a local media frenzy ensued. Unfortunately, they had a problem getting out of England at Heathrow Airport because Johnny Rotten was an asshole to the customs official. They arrived in America a day late. The show was supposed to be rescheduled, but the tour fell apart (as did the band) and they went back to the U.K.

8. Hall & Oates: The Agora was having a problem with the fire marshal for overcrowding. The group had sold out both shows (seven and ten o'clock). The first show was in progress and there were a thousand people lined up on the sidewalk waiting to get in for the second show. The fire marshal shows up and demands to stop the show, put on the lights, and count heads. Knowing that it would cause a riot, our front-door guard (a Cleveland cop) claimed that the fire marshal bumped him, arrested him for assaulting an officer, and hustled him into the office, where he was held until they could transport him to jail (about four hours later). The real show that night was in the lobby.

7. Bad Company: I watched this entire show from the wings, stage right. It was amazing how Paul Rodgers had the crowd in the palm

I think it was about six dates. I still run across people who remember it. It was so phenomenal because they had all those hits—they were doing "My Girl," "The Way You Do the Things You Do," "Beauty's Only Skin Deep"—this is before they got to the psychedelic stuff.

The only thing the Temptations don't have, they don't have the nitty-gritty, gutbucket, R&B ballad songs that make you get the blues and cry in your beer, and we had those kinds of songs. We got a song from Wilson Pickett, "Midnight Hour," did an Eddie Floyd song; the O'Jays had a song called "Stand In for Love," and we decided we were going to open up with this song, and the first line is "I'm like a shadow in the dark/I can't be seen." We opened up with the stage completely black, and I'm not the lightest-skinned guy. There I am in pitch black and I come out with "I'm like a shadow in the dark," with the background vocals. And then the light hits, it was on from then on. We opened up on a Wednesday; by the time we got to Sunday, we had to get steroid shots, we'd sung so hard. It was one of the best gigs I ever did in my life, and I became a huge Temptations fan from then on, because I understood they were the real thing. —**Eddie Levert, musician (the O'Jays)**

My first experience at singing was at Leo's. I peed on myself, I was so scared. I kept telling my dad, I wanna sing, I wanna sing. My mother was working as a nurse at the time. So I was a little kid looking up women's skirts, doing crazy stuff like that. One night, they were doing a show and I got up there, got ready to sing. I got nervous because the crowd was getting all excited; he was holding me, and I was singing up to the mike, and I knew all of the songs because I was there every night, because he had to babysit me at night. I remember him just being frantic, having to run offstage and change clothes. I stood there and cried. I was a little kid, I thought I was going to be a star. —**Gerald Levert, musician (and son of Eddie Levert)**

La Cave was a different kind of place. The small, narrow basement room held 250. It ran from 1952 to 1969, showcased nearly every act on the Elektra label, and, like Club 47 in Cambridge, Massachusetts, the Troubadour in Los Angeles, and New York's Bitter End, served up legendary performances. Neil Young informed Daffy Dan this was his last club date because he was going with Crosby, Stills & Nash; Blood, Sweat & Tears star Al Kooper warned people there might be a narc in the audience; and several say that one of James Cotton's drummers died mid-performance.

The only place you could go to hear folk music was La Cave in Cleveland or this place called the Left Bank at University Circle. Left Bank was the only place where beatniks hung out—the coffee-drinking, cigarette-smok-

of his hand. When they did their last song, "Can't Get Enough of Your Love" it was positively electrifying.

6. Paul Simon: He spent six weeks at the club filming his movie *One Trick Pony.* They used my office as the set for the club manager's office in the flick because they liked all the stuff I had on my walls. After days of rehearsing, someone on their crew found the sub-basement in the club (we called it the dungeon) and decided that it looked grittier, with its dirt and exposed pipes. That's the one that appears in the movie. The Simon concert in the movie was obviously filmed on our stage before a real crowd and featured some of the best New York session cats.

5. Elvis Costello: His first tour of the States. This was one of the shows underwritten by the record company, designed to break him in front of a Cleveland audience. The tickets were $1.01 and, of course, presented by WMMS, which is at 101 on the dial. The performance was astounding, with its fast tempos and rapid-fire cadence, but once again, the real show was in the dressing room, where Hank LoConti almost got into a fistfight with Jake Riviera, Costello's manager, who was apparently trying to teach Elvis how to be an "angry young man" by being a raging asshole.

4. The Clash: These were punks who could play. Their album "London Calling" was zooming up the charts. They were ushering in a new era in rock music. Out with the old guard and in with the new thing. On the morning of the show, their manager called me to say that Joe Strummer had a terrible toothache, and could I take him to the dentist. I drove him to my dentist, who fixed him up and the show went on. Later my dentist told me that those were the worst teeth he had ever seen.

3. Southside Johnny and the Asbury Jukes: They were the perfect Cleveland band—the ultimate bar band.

On this night, we were videotaping them for a TV show that we had for one season called *Onstage at the Agora*. It was a four-camera shoot and we had one take to get it. It was set to broadcast that week. On the same night, Bruce Springsteen was playing at the Coliseum. When Bruce's show ended, he got in a van and came to the Agora to jam with Southside. He jumped onstage and the crowd went berserk. Bruce played and sang on the band's last three songs. It was complete pandemonium, all the while with the cameras rolling. I was thinking, "Now *this* is a TV show!"

Then the next day, Hank got a call from Bruce's manager, Jon Landau, who said, "By the way, you can't use the footage of Bruce." It seems Bruce had never done a video before and they didn't want his first one to be this jam thing. We were obviously very disappointed, especially because now the Southside TV show had no closing climax. Every act saves their strongest, most exciting songs for the finale. In this case, we weren't able to use Southside's sweaty, rave-up ending.

2. Meat Loaf with opening act Tom Petty: Steve Popovich discovered Meat Loaf and signed him to his label. Steve wanted to break him out of Cleveland and wanted to play the Agora circuit. I booked the first four concerts Meat ever played, and I got a gold record out of it. The concert was a young, hungry Meat Loaf at his best. His operatic histrionics were that of a crazy man. He was wild-eyed. He collapsed backstage after the encore. Oh yeah, Tom Petty opened.

1. Bruce Springsteen and the E Street Band: Bruce . . . in a club . . . up close and personal . . . for $7.50. Actually, the record company bought all the tickets and WMMS gave them away on the radio. It was the tenth-anniversary celebration of the radio station. The show was broadcast live to radio stations in ten other cities . . . a simulcast

ing beatnik. Then La Cave opened up playing folk music and was where you started to see the progression from beatnik to hippie. I saw Ian and Sylvia, I saw Paul Butterfield, I saw the group that changed me musically, took me to progressive music—the Blues Project—and Al Kooper with Blood, Sweat & Tears; Al Kooper played there a lot. La Cave was a club, a real club. Leo's was later, Leo's was like '65, '66, '67. Leo's was about Motown, that's what made Leo's famous. But the whole scene developed out of La Cave. That transition from Top 40 to what was then called underground or progressive music happened in Cleveland because of La Cave; this is where you first heard of these things. —**Billy Bass, DJ**

"Leo's was about Motown, that's what made Leo's famous. But the whole scene developed out of La Cave."

La Cave seemed illicit because it was a very grown-up, very college kind of thing. The band I remember most distinctly was Terry Knight and the Pack. They were great . . . I remember [also] the other people I saw at La Cave—what was that woman's name? Odetta. There was Bob Gibson. Those people were complete folkies—the smoky room kind of drinking coffee type of thing. But Terry Knight and the Pack were real rockers; I remember distinctly going to see them three or four times at La Cave. For some reason, they mixed with the rest of that talent. I remember I had a girlfriend who just loved Terry Knight. He was real, oh, fancy boy, sex symbol kind of thing. Mick Jagger kind of presence. If you saw him walking down the street, it would be oh, who's this guy? But when he's onstage, he oozes that sexuality. It was more than my girlfriend; it was my first wife, now that I mention it. She wanted to go there just to see him gyrate. I don't think she was into his music at all, though she professed to be. —**Ed Watkins, fan (North Olmsted)**

I was still fairly straight, I was wearing J. Press suits and making some decent money, and my program director, Bob Conrad, WCLV, invited me to see Judy Collins at the only folk club, La Cave. The neighborhood was on its way to being a torn-down ghetto in those days. We went, we took our wives, we're the only people in the place wearing ties. Judy Collins came out with Spike Lee's father [Bill Lee] playing bass, and she completely knocked me out. I was sitting an inch away from her, and she was gorgeous and her voice was unbelievable and she sang all these wonderful songs. So we went backstage, and there was Bill Lee smoking a spliff the size of my arm. I met Judy, I felt a connection with her. The next day her record label, Elektra, asked me to do a record signing in the Cleveland Heights store [Discount Records] with her. I said, wow—I said, fine. —**Martin Perlich, former WMMS DJ**

Leo's Casino was originally located at East 49th Street and Central Avenue; after a fire there in 1963, it moved to the Quad Hall hotel at 75th and Euclid and finally closed in 1972.

Leo's closed basically because the white audience from the suburbs didn't want to come there. Leo's is often thought of as a black club, but its audience was 60 percent white; the bread and butter was white audiences. There were the '66 Hough riots and '68 Glenville disturbances. A perception started to occur that once you got past University Circle, the city wasn't as safe as it once was. La Cave followed Leo's because those white audiences weren't coming down. There was no more live touring name entertainment in Cleveland. It was a very dark time. —**Larry Bruner, manager of La Cave 1966–69**

"The bread and butter was white audiences."

A mid-performance death took place at La Cave, according to three eyewitnesses, and Bruner affirms it.

It was a very, very dark place, it was a very, very hip type of place. When you walked in, you thought you were entering another world. With people waiting in line, musicians would walk down the same staircase . . . [James Cotton's] drummer had a heart attack and died that night. The whole drum kit keeled over; the whole band stopped playing. People thought it was a joke at first; the whole band was hovering around, people soon realized this wasn't a joke. The cops or medics came in, took him to the hospital, I think it was St. Alexis, where he died.

After they took him away, they continued to play. James Cotton took over the drums. He'd been playing with Muddy Waters; this was his own band. His guitar player was Luther Tucker; he thought he was going to be the next B.B. King. —**Carl Gonzalez, fan (Bay Village)**

I believe the drummer's name was Bill Stepney. My two guitar players at that time were waiters at La Cave, so I had carte blanche down there; we used to rehearse after hours . . . The drummer had high blood pressure; he loved to drink tea brewed from marijuana. He slipped me a cup of tea. I

. . . that means no overdubs, no fixing flubs, just live music as it happens. Bruce walked in and asked if we had three eight-foot banquet tables. The stagehands produced them and Bruce had his crew nail them perpendicular to the stage . . . one on the left, one on the right, and one in the middle. He now had three ramps that he, Miami Steve, and Clarence Clemons could use to run out into the crowd on cue. They played for four hours. It was THE BEST CONCERT EVER HELD AT THE AGORA.

A COMMUNITY OF COOL:

The Velvet Underground played seven shows at La Cave, including one that was recorded but never officially released.

Cleveland's Notable Rock and Roll Venues of the 1970s

Admiral Bilbo's, Center Ridge Rd., Westlake
Agora (on E. 24th St.)
Akron Rubber Bowl
Blossom Music Center
Bobby McGee's (across from the Palace)
Chesterland Hullabaloo
Cleveland Arena
Clockwork Orange, Payne Ave.
Cloverleaf Speedway, Valley View
Cock N Bull, Payne Ave.
Cyrus Erie West
Dealer's Choice, Maple Hts.
Fat Glenn's (on the campus of Cleveland State near Music Grotto)
The Flipside, Noble and Mayfield roads in Cleveland Hts.
Friar Tuck's, Kent
Front Row Theater, Highland Hts.
Grapes of Wrath, across the street from the Viking on Chester Ave.
Hennessy's, Lakewood (later the Hi-Fi Club)
Horrigan's Bar, Shaker Hts.
House of Bud, Euclid Ave.
J.B.'s., Kent
Jicky's English Disco, E. 30th and Euclid Ave., at the Piccadilly
Kaleidoscope, on Payne Ave. (west of the Agora)
The Kove, Kent
The Loaded Lounge, E. 18th and Payne Ave.
Longhorn, Maple Hts. (also known as Mr. Magoo's)
The Lower Level (formerly Hire's Lounge)
The Mistake (basement of Agora on E. 24th St.)
Municipal Stadium
Musicarnival, Warrensville Hts.
Otto Site

tasted it, it had this funny aftertaste—fifteen, twenty minutes later, you're getting a little mellow. To get back to the actual story, they're doing "Sweet 16," a B.B. King song, the drummer was getting slower and slower, his arms were getting higher and higher, all of a sudden he stands up, pitches forward, and knocks the drum set over. A fellow I knew a couple tables away thought it was part of the act, stood up and applauded. They took the drummer to the side and laid him down, and EMS came about twenty minutes later and took him out. He died—and Cotton came back and finished the night playing drums and harmonica and everything else. —**Bill Miller, musician (Mr. Stress Blues Band)**

I'm sure it was after he'd been there a couple of days, and I'm almost positive it was a Sunday. It really wasn't a dramatic thing; it's not every day that you see a drummer just fall over, but that's basically what it was. Cotton was playing; I can't remember how many pieces there were—it had be a bass player, drummer, guitar player, and harp. It's like a vague thing; I was there but I can't tell you exactly what happened. There were not that many people there, relatively speaking, it was a moderate-sized crowd. It came to an end, people were sort of stunned, and they left.

I subsequently found out that he died but I didn't know he was dead at the time. And I can't tell you the drummer's name, none of that stuff, it's just vague. The only thing I really remember is a lot of green hue colors, I don't know why. Green was the predominant color, not the color I normally associated with La Cave. But it did happen, that's all I can tell you. —**Andrew Axilrod, fan (Philadelphia)**

For those with a bit of energy left, there was after-hours entertainment:

After your job you'd go to Chung Wah's at East 36th and St. Clair. The place was full of pimps and hookers and local bands. People were generally pretty drunk or high, the waitresses heard a lot of jokes about flied lice, they were probably getting a lot of abuse. This one night I was there with the guys from Dragonwyck. We had a table of like twenty people from different bands. Everybody was shooting the breeze and there was this pimp who was wearing this pair of electric green pants, and he had a floppy collar and a three-quarter-length black coat and a green hat with a wide brim. He was standing there to pick up some food to go. And this Caddy that was that electric metallic green they used to make in a DeVille was outside. He was completely pimped out.

And some altercation happened, something to do with the check. They had one little guy who always rang the register, and while they were arguing the pimp made his point. And he made a big gesture of pulling his coat back to show he had a piece in his waistband, he had a gun. And the guy behind the register went like, a guttural two words, and out of the kitchen came a guy wearing a low toque with an apron, and he had a sword, and he squatted in the heron's pose where you put the point towards the person, and said a word, and our guy goes, "Motherfucker comes out with a sword, these guys are fucking crazy," and he walked out. That was the end of it. And I thought, here's a guy in front of me with a sword, forget about it. That just went to tell you, the shit people are dealing out to them, they're pretty good-natured. But somebody's going to come out here with a sword.

This is 1972, probably over the winter, it would have been 2 A.M., middle of the night. And everybody's sitting there in their own little world going, okay, guess we won't be running out on the check here, will we? I wonder what he said. —**Dale Flanigan, musician (Dragonwyck)**

"The place was full of pimps and hookers and local bands. People were generally pretty drunk or high."

Here's a close call from the Allen Theatre, a popular venue in the early '70s, where the Stampeders, famous only for "Sweet City Woman," opened for Mountain in fall '74:

Two of the guys wandered in off the street asking where they could get any weed. So we have all this trash in the theater, we had to blow all the trash to the front of the stage, then sweep it up. We were saying we don't have any, but if you look down here, you'll probably find some. So we go down there and started digging around, found a joint—they were skeptical, but said, hey, I found one too. Then we kind of hung around with these guys for a while, so they wanted to score, we were able to hook 'em up with somebody the next day, the day they played.

We had an awful problem with people trying to sneak in through the garage at the back of the theater; they had built an addition to it and had covered over some of the dressing-room windows. So we were in this dressing room with these guys, these guys are Canadians, they had this bag of weed and put it in one of those metal towel dispensers because they were paranoid about holding it. So they took a bunch of the paper towels out of the dispenser and shoved this baggie underneath there and shoved the towels back

- Peabody's Cafe, Cedar and Taylor roads, Cleveland Hts.
- Peabody's in the Flats (the former Pirate's Cove)
- Pirate's Cove
- Public Hall
- Richfield Coliseum
- The Road South
- The Scalded Frog, Mentor Ave., Painesville
- Smiling Dog, W. 25th St. by I-90
- Socrates' Cave (later the Mad Hatter)
- Studio B
- Swingo's, E. 18th and Euclid Ave.
- The Symposium, Lakewood
- Tap Room
- Utopia, Euclid Ave. (formerly the Orbit Lounge) Willoughby
- Viking Saloon

Cleveland's Notable Rock and Roll Venues of the 1980s

- Agora (E. 24th St.)
- Akron Rubber Bowl
- Blossom Music Center
- Dixie Electric Company (where a drummer played along with the DJ)
- The Flipside
- Friar Tuck's, Kent
- Front Row Theater
- J.B.'s, Kent
- Pop Shop (after the Mistake)
- Cloverleaf Speedway
- The Flipside
- The Lower Level, Euclid Ave., Wickliffe
- Municipal Stadium
- The Music Machine, Parma
- Peabody's in the Flats (the former Pirate's Cove)
- Richfield Coliseum
- Swingo's, E. 18th and Euclid Ave.
- Traxx (DJs only)

in. Some kid was trying to climb through the window, I was like, hey man, get the hell out of here, and he got mouthy.

This kid kind of left, but then a policeman came in the room unexpectedly, looked out the window, and got his hands all dirty. There's a sink there, he starts washing his hands. He needs something to dry them on, and these guys are going, here, use these towels. The policeman's real nice, I'm sure he knew what we were doing back there. He's saying, I'll just start using these paper ones, starts pulling out towels from the dispensers on the wall, these guys are like frozen with fear. He pulled out a few towels, dried his hands, walked away. He came within three or four inches of where the bag of weed was. —**Frank Dutton, former Allen Theatre worker**

At the Allen Theatre [June 14, 1974], we had the New York Dolls with David Johansen and they of course dressed outlandish, with big red lips, high heels and dresses, and they were the headliners. And Kiss was the opening act. And one of the girls from Belkin said, I want you to meet Gene Simmons, and of course, he is so tall, with those boots on especially, and I looked up. I had never seen Kiss, I went, uh, uh, but that's my name. (Simmons is my maiden name.) I said, I've never met anybody with my name, especially who looked like you. He laughed.

You know how Gene Simmons spouts that fire? He has those torches onstage. Peter Kriss is on the drum stand and all the other guys are out front on microphone. We're standing on these spiral staircases watching the show from the wings. Around the border of Kriss's stand there's fringe; the drum set is on this hydraulic lift, and during one of the songs, the set starts rising. As it's going up, it's wiggling, so the fringe is going back and forth and catches on fire from one of these torches. And the fringe is burning very quickly, and it's starting to burn all around the drum set, which is on this wooden plank. It's one of those scenes where they put the missionary in the pot.

Peter Kriss did not miss a drumbeat. None of the guys in front of us see this, of course. We're yelling behind the stage, Fire, fire! And of course nobody hears us, it's so loud. We're in this old wooden movie theater, 1921, which if it caught fire would probably cause a lot of damage. We had to run down the staircase and into the alley, where the stagehands are having smokes, say the stage is on fire. A guy runs in with one of those big CO2 extinguishers, blasts it all around and puts out the fire during the show. The other guys are all up front and still playing, they don't know this. They turn around and see all this and all the kids in the audience start standing up and cheering. They thought it was part of the show. —**Jeannie Emser, publicist**

When it came to promoting shows in Cleveland, the Belkins ruled:

The Belkin brothers were just starting out, so we went to Jules, said all we want to do is call it WIXY Presents, get our disc jockey to introduce the act, we'll promote it for you. They agreed, and we did dozens of appearances. We eventually got the Belkins to buy some time, too. We even had a big poster made that said "WIXY 1260 Presents," then we'd have Jack Armstrong get up onstage, say WIXY Brings You . . . we got the halo effect from bringing in these acts, from Belkin Productions. When they started out, Belkin didn't mean anything because they were behind the scenes and WIXY was out front.

The Belkins were very, very good promoters. We had seen other promoters come and go and one of the reasons the promotion business was unstable was that a lot of unstable people were in it; the Belkins were very different, they were good businessmen. If they made money on an act, they'd put it in the bank and have a cushion for the next time. To have a conservative guy in the promotion business was new and unique for that time. —**Norman Wain, WIXY co-founder**

"A lot of unstable people were in [this business]. The Belkins were very different, they were good businessmen."

The Belkins saw the value of the dollar from their very first show February 5, 1966. It was the Four Freshmen with the Christy Minstrels at Music Hall.

I had already made previous arrangements to take a vacation, so I wasn't even there. At the end of the evening, the first show did not do well, so it didn't bode well for the second show, but for some reason people came out for the second show, so we made $57 for the evening. Compared to what we would have to do in the clothing business—socks in those days were 39 cents a pair—to clear $57, we said, you know what? This is a pretty good business. So we said, let's go on from there. —**Jules Belkin, promoter**

FROM SOCKS TO ROCK: Jules and Michael Belkin worked in their family's downtown Cleveland clothing store until the mid '60s. In the years to come, the duo would go on to book some of the biggest shows in Cleveland as well as manage the Michael Stanley Band.

Paul Revere and the Raiders—a favorite group on "Upbeat."

FANNING THE FLAMES

Music and the Media

Cleveland's radio personalities had signatures, like Alan Freed's Moondog howl, Murray Saul's "Get down," and Kid Leo's voice, a unique blend of the dulcet and the dirty. There have been signature TV personalities, too, like Don Webster, the affable host of *Upbeat,* the show Herman Spero and his son, David, ran Saturday afternoons at 5 over Channel 5. And let's not forget that "kicky" *Plain Dealer* scribe Jane Scott.

"Upbeat" Rules

Even though it ran only from 1964 to 1971, *Upbeat* lingers in Cleveland memory. The reasons are its house bands—from Joey and the Continentals to the Grasshoppers to the Outsiders—its stars, and Webster, the Canadian boy who engaged Cleveland audiences so effortlessly.

What WIXY was to WMMS, *Upbeat* was to *American Bandstand*—or, more accurately, MTV. It ultimately ran in 110 markets across the U.S. It showcased popular and up-and-coming artists, snagging them as they passed through town to play the many clubs and other venues that featured rock and roll in the '60s and '70s. *Upbeat* was the show where Simon and Garfunkel made their first TV appearance and where Otis Redding made his last. The following morning, December 10, 1967, he died in a plane crash, along with his band, the Bar-Kays.

HERMAN SPERO PRODUCTIONS, INC.

6337

SOCIETY NATIONAL BANK OF CLEVELAND, CLEVELAND, OHIO

PAID DEC 28 '67

Hundred & Eight & 00/100 DOLLARS

PAY TO THE ORDER OF

12/9/67 Otis Red[illegible] 6-103

Upbeat 12/9/67

HERMAN SPERO PRODUCTIONS, INC.

⑈0410⑆0103⑈ 050⑉5464⑈ ⑆0000020800⑆

A SAD PAYDAY:
This is the check Otis Redding signed for his Dec. 9, 1967 performance on *Upbeat*. That night he played Leo's Casino. The next day, he and his backup band, the Bar-Kays, died in a plane crash.

"He did *Upbeat* on Saturday, Leo's Casino on Saturday night, and he died on Sunday," said David Spero, whose father produced *Upbeat.*

There were other, related TV shows, like the *Friedman Buick Dance Party* Norman Wain hosted at 11 A.M. Saturdays on Channel 5 in the late '50s. The R&B answer to *Upbeat* was *The Big K* hosted by Ken Hawkins of WJMO. According to Tom Feran, a columnist at the *Plain Dealer,* it was based on *American Bandstand* and featured local black kids dancing to records, with Hawkins hosting and interviewing acts. (The audience on *Upbeat* stayed in the bleachers and didn't go out to dance at all. The dancing was done originally by the Dick

Blake Dancers and later the Jeff Kutash Dancers.) Channel 3's version was *The Jerry G Show*, which became *The Big Ralph Show* hosted by Jay Lawrence after Jerry G left town. It ran early Saturday evening. They'd spotlight a different high school every week, and about ten kids from the school would be featured dancers while they counted down the week's top ten tunes.

Upbeat is the show we remember.

BORN TO DANCE:

Bev Jones was one of the Upbeat dancers, along with Sandy Ashmun (the future Mrs. Barry Gabel).

"They'd spotlight a different high school every week, and about ten kids from the school would be featured dancers."

I think the show was started two weeks before I got there, only because I came from Canada and I was hung up on immigration getting across the border. When we were just local, we were tied up with WHK radio, and we'd have the disc jockeys from HK come in and co-host. They brought in Joe Mayer, Bob Friend, Johnny Walters, and there was one more. We used to have Terry Knight and the Pack on. Terry's dead now. [Knight was fatally stabbed in November 2004.] All the people from Motown used to stop in Cleveland when they had a new record because being so close to Detroit, they'd make their first tour stop in Cleveland. Berry Gordy trained them well, these people were really great to work with. You could tell a Motown group right away because they all moved the same way. Smokey Robinson was one, and Martha Reeves was another one. They were all equally good.

We used a band called the Grasshoppers for a while; Benny Orr [Parma's Benny Orzechowski, dead of cancer in October 2000] was the lead singer who went on to big things [as lead singer of the Cars]. Dave C and the Sharptones was our first house band. Another guy was Stevie Wonder. He was another one who was just completely professional. On the other hand, I remember we had Eric Burdon from the Animals, he was probably one of the most difficult interviews I've ever done. Yup, nope. He didn't want to talk. He wanted to do his thing and get it over with. —**Don Webster, former *Upbeat* host**

I was on TV for dancing, on the *Jerry G Show*, he had all this crap going on. He did a show for about a year on Channel 3 to compete with *Upbeat*, it was Saturday nights, an hour. He had national acts and then he got all local high school kids to dance: This week we got Normandy, next week we got Parma. St. Joe's picked the best dancers and I was one of them. —**Chuck Rambaldo, fan (North Royalton)**

Herman Spero wanted to bring Top 40 AM radio to television. His son says it was the first rock and roll show "that wasn't a dance party."

He wanted to do Top 40 on TV, so in the same hour, you could have Tommy James, the Supremes, Ramsey Lewis, Duke Ellington, and Bobby Goldsboro and five other acts. The reason he was able to get such a volume of different artists was because of the club scene that was going on. There was La Cave, where he would get Simon and Garfunkel, Blood, Sweat & Tears, and the Blues Project. Up the street was Leo's Casino, where he could get the Temptations, the Four Tops, or Otis Redding. There were some jazz clubs around Cleveland that had people like Dizzy Gillespie, like the Theatrical, or a Doc Severinsen or Gene Krupa. And then there was the Cleveland Grande Ballroom, the WHK Auditorium, at 50th and Euclid, now the Agora, and you could have Deep Purple or the Moody Blues. And we had a thriving concert scene. —**David Spero, fan (South Euclid)**

EARTH TO DON:

David Spero cues *Upbeat* MC Don Webster.

Early R&B had a lot of musicians that had jazz in their background. A lot of rock cats who grew up in the '50s and '60s took lessons with jazz guys, many with the initial thought of playing that music. Life and circumstances led them to the rock side. Don Kubec and I played in bands together (like the house band at Leo's Casino), but as the '60s continued he became more and more committed to the rock of that era and began to play with Buddy Maver in a band called Charade, which was quite successful in the era. That is the way it was for many musicians of that time. I played with a jazz arranger/trumpet player named Tom Baker in the early part of the '60s in Tom's jazz quintet. Tom became the contractor for Leo's and hired me (of course). Like some jazz musicians I played in pit bands and did recording sessions because musicianship (if not improvisational ability) was in demand.

I think the entire stable of Motown acts played Leo's during our tenure there. The Supremes, the Temptations, Martha and the Vandellas, the Four Tops, Smokey Robinson, Marvin Gaye, etc. all played there a number of times. My favorite group was the O'Jays (from Canton). They were regulars at Leo's and in the beginning they were pure R&B. They had the best and funkiest rhythm section going, David Johnson on bass, Jerry Baxter on drums, Russell Evans on guitar, and Richard Shann on keyboards. Always a fan of music that grooves, I loved the weeks that the O'Jays played, and later I did some jazz/funk gigs with that rhythm section.

Don Webster hosted *Upbeat*, but he wasn't the only star. The Upbeat Dancers gave him quite a lift every Saturday at 5 p.m.

Tom Baker became passionate about the Motown sound, took up bass (he sounded just like Jimmie Jamerson), and got into arranging and eventually producing pop/rock and R&B recording sessions. Tom became music director for Terry Knight who had left the Pack and was looking to broaden his musical horizons (and his audience base). Tom hired me to be part of the four pieces that were permanent to the Terry Knight Revue. We would pick up four other horn players (from various cities) and play a mix of R&B, pop, with a touch (just a small touch) of jazz.

Tom would go on to be music director of *Upbeat*. The house band for the show was the GTOs, a group that performed in the local clubs. They were led by Joey Porrello and were originally known as Joey and the Continentals, a dynamite early '60s rock group that was a big favorite of young Cleveland dancers. I also took part in sessions that Tom Baker produced for the GTO's, Terry Knight, the O'Jays ("Backstabbers" and "Lipstick Traces"), and the Outsiders. The Outsiders were led by Tom King, who earlier in the '60s led a group called Tom King and the Starfires. I briefly played with them when the group's drummer was Jim Fox, later of James Gang fame. Sonny Geraci, the Outsiders' lead singer, has a brother named Mike, a fine tenor player who played in a rock group [Rastus] in the '70s that had an unusual, for the genre at that time, two-tenor-sax tandem as a horn section.

In the '70s jazz players incorporated many of the trappings and sounds of the rock music of that era. At the Smiling Dog Saloon all the music came together. Almost every act in jazz played there, as well as many rock and folk acts. I played the club as leader of the house band for many of the jazz acts. I also played there with the Bill DeArango Trio. Bill was the legendary jazz guitarist who at about this time was incorporating the direction opened up by Jimi Hendrix in a "free music" group with me and drummer Skip Hadden. People were describing our music as "Heavy Metal Jazz." We were very controversial and very rock influenced. —**Ernie Krivda, musician**

TALK ABOUT ECLECTIC:

People associate the Smiling Dog Saloon with jazz, but it was much more. These 1973 ads prove the Dog did just about every kind of music.

Meanwhile, at Channel 5:

Anybody who came through town who was playing Leo's Casino always played the show—Dionne Warwick, those people. James Brown was on several times with his entourage. I was there to dance and it was just fun to get paid doing this on a Saturday, when you're in high school. We did routines sometimes that were to certain songs, occasionally it was with a band that was performing. There was the Ohio Teen Fair at Chippewa Lake, we had Gary Lewis & the Playboys; my guess would be this was 1966, but when I cut these clippings out, or my mother or grandmother did, we didn't necessarily think to save the date. Also on that date were Mitch Ryder and the Detroit Wheels—and all the midway rides were free.

When it changed from *The Big 5* to *Upbeat* I first met Jane Scott. She always had that same look with the glasses, like she just happened to be in the right spot, like she walked in the front door but knew what was going on.

I remember Bob Seger being on and he was very bizarre at the time, wearing some woolly kind of vest thing, his song was "Heavy Music," there was a lot of controversy around, the same as the Stones' "Satisfaction." It seems funny in today's world that anyone questioned those songs.

One of my best friends and I danced on the show together, and then we would get hired to do private shows, like bar mitzvahs. It wasn't so much glamorous as it was more exciting than working the Dairy Queen. I think we used to get like $25 a show, but we were doing stuff that we would have been doing just for fun anyway.

"It wasn't so much glamorous as it was more exciting than working the Dairy Queen."

The Versaille Motor Inn across from Channel 5 was considered the entertainers' hotel. I think it also attracted a certain type of person who might hang out in the lobby. I was wearing my little white high school dress and waiting for Jeff Kutash, the *Upbeat* choreographer, and this older gentleman tried to convince me not to have a life of crime; he thought I was a hooker. It took me a while to figure out what he thought I was doing there, he was going to give me money just to leave. I remember thinking how obnoxious all these performers were. We actually did date some of the guys; we were so innocent, we just hung out and had fun, it was very innocent dating, not like the groupies of today—from my end of it anyway.

—**Sam Gabel, former *Upbeat* dancer**

Don Webster interviews the Monkees' Davy Jones and Mickey Dolenz.

Fashion Cues

My most vivid memory of *Upbeat* was seeing the Music Machine for the first time, and I thought they were way cool; they all wore the one black leather glove, which was real kind of outlawish. I remember going to Federal's Department Store the next day and I paid $3.49 for that record. I'm going to guess this was 1965, '66. The big song was "Talk, Talk." On *Upbeat* they played "The People and Me," my favorite song on the whole record. The Music Machine all had the black, shaggy hair, the black leather pants, the single leather glove, they were very menacing looking. Of course the songs were all lip synched back then; you kind of knew it, but it was still kind of a cool show to see. —**Chris Jacobs, fan (Rocky River)**

Don Webster (left) and Billy Bass bracket the popular Bobby Goldsboro during an *Upbeat* appearance.

Like WIXY, *Upbeat* was incredibly popular:

The ratings were phenomenal at five o'clock on Saturday. The way that worked, we taped on Saturday—that was before satellite, it was two-inch tape, and we would send it out; I think about six months after it started we went to the other stations in the Scripps Howard chain and shortly after that we were in syndication. The show would play at five o'clock in Cleveland, then we'd ship out ten tapes to the biggest stations in New York, Chicago, and L.A., and the next week they would ship those tapes out to other stations. You got to hit ten cities, you're talking ten weeks. That was really a great thing for performers, and there was nothing on around the country. We really started that type of programming. The record companies loved the exposure. If we wanted a big act, the record companies would say you could have the big act, but you gotta take this new kid.

I just thought that it was really a lot of fun, going out every week and doing it. The funny thing is, we worked with all kinds of people who are now in the Rock and Roll Hall of Fame. I remember Lesley Gore always traveled with her mother. I remember NBC was on strike and Ed McMahon made a record with Lesley, he came in and co-hosted the show with me. I don't think I ever looked better. He was the best second banana I've ever seen in my life, the way he used to do with Johnny all the time.

James Brown ran one of the tightest ships you've ever seen. He would come in with a band, we'd rehearse, maybe run over something again, and right after lunch, and the next hour. He kept a book on everybody. He'd fine them if they weren't there; those guys really jumped when he said jump. He would travel with his own band.

Sly and the Family Stone was on, and he always wore outlandish clothing. He was on time. Those were the days when everybody smoked heavily. I mean grass rather than cigarettes. We had a group who were all buzzed and did a rehearsal in the morning and by the time it came to doing the show they were gone. I think they thought they'd done it, you know?

Another great, great guy who went on to big things and kind of disappeared was Bobby Sherman. He was in L.A. working with the LAPD, some kind of EMS guy . . .

What I miss about it is that during that time, there was some really good

music being written. The Beatles, that type of thing. Before the end of the show was when that heavy metal music started. A neat thing about it was how we were rock primarily but we still had different kinds of people on, like Dizzy Gillespie was on, Gene Krupa was on. I remember Paul Anka coming in; he didn't do much television. You set him down to a piano, he'd do a whole thing. He has five daughters, he lived in some little town in California, never wanted to raise his family in Hollywood. Jane Scott was there every week. She covered everybody. Jane Scott can tell you more things about who was in what group. She was just an encyclopedia. Probably still is.
—**Don Webster, former *Upbeat* host**

"Those were the days when everybody smoked heavily. I mean grass rather than cigarettes."

Great Scott!

Jane Scott, who was born May 3, 1919 (the same day as Pete Seeger), looms as large in Cleveland rock lore as any performer. Among the highlights of her career: missing the Moondog Coronation Ball in 1952; interviewing the Beatles in 1966; hanging out backstage with everybody from Elvis Costello (not so nice) to Lyle Lovett (very, very nice). Scott retired in 2002 after fifty years at the *Plain Dealer*. When she broke her hip in January 2006, one *Plain Dealer* columnist sent her an online valentine on Cleveland.com:

> I met Jane Scott I think four times . . . First time, about thirty-five years ago . . . she interviewed me, a lowly kid journalist, about the state of Cleveland AM rock radio! Her interviewing me made my family's month, not day! The PD clipping with her byline is still in a scrapbook somewhere with a photo of teen me. She made me feel important. Her status (her audience with the Beatles, etc.), that's what did it for me as a teen. —**Sarah Crump, *Plain Dealer* columnist**

THE PEOPLE'S ROCK REPORTER: Count on Jane Scott to be at every rock show, pen and notepad at the ready.

A graduate of Lakewood High School, the University of Michigan, and the defunct Wilcox College of Commerce on Public Square, Scott became known in the '50s for her work as teen writer and golden age writer—covering everything "from pimples to pensions." She is an unabashed fan who always accentuates the positive.

My theory is I am here to be the eyes and ears of young people, especially those who can't afford or have the opportunity to go to where they really want to go . . . if I hate it or love it, they don't give a damn. They don't care. I don't like the Beastie Boys, but I don't say that. I don't see any reason to like them, but anyway . . . I try to put it from their standpoint or point of view, and if you have attitude, you're not just writing for yourself: Oh, I love this, I love that. I give them a chance. I think everybody deserves a chance, even the ones that are the fringe players. They deserve a little something; you never know, they might turn out to be somebody big, too. Bruce Springsteen opened for Wishbone Ash at the Allen; I try to live by that. I have to be honest, though. I can judge what I think of their music; some of it is really trash, I admit it. But very rarely. We're writing for our readers, too. I don't puff it up at all. I just do it as honestly as I can. But I loved the Beatles; they were nice to me when I was there. . . .

"Some of it is really trash, I admit it. But very rarely."

I was the *Plain Dealer*'s teen editor when I attended the Beatles' first concert in Cleveland, on Sept. 15, 1964, at Public Hall. Two years later, I became the paper's rock critic and covered the Beatles' second show here—at a much larger venue, the Stadium.

The latter was one of the top cultural events in Cleveland history and one of the most exciting days in my nearly 30 years as a Plain Dealer rock critic. Memorable moments have also been provided by other Rock and Roll Hall of Fame inductees—notably the Rolling Stones, Janis Joplin and Jimi Hendrix—and many others.

The Beatles' session for reporters at the old Hotel Cleveland Sheraton the day of their concert on Aug. 14, 1966, was my first major news conference. It was about as easy to get into as the Michael Jackson–Lisa Marie Presley honeymoon suite. Even Beatles Manager Brian Epstein was denied entrance at first. Luckily, Norman Wain, co-owner of concert sponsor WIXY AM, got me in. —**Jane Scott, music critic**

WHO'S THAT WITH JANE?

Jane Scott interviewed just about everyone. Here she is with: Sting, Billy Joel, David Bowie, and Peter Gabriel.

Scott wrote that for the *Plain Dealer* on August 28, 1995. The press conference before that 1966 concert was the one time she got a chance to speak with Lennon. She'd prepped by traveling to Liverpool to research the Beatles in 1965, the year they didn't make it to Cleveland because of a ban by Mayor Ralph Locher. She recalls the interview at the old Sheraton Hotel:

I met them and so did the man from Channel 5, and Brian [Epstein] was there, of course. You know how they had those big microphones? They stuck them in Paul McCartney's face and I couldn't get a word in so I was forced to talk to John Lennon. Paul was so cute, you know. I didn't know until later that was the only time I could talk to him. After the '66 show, that was it; the next time you heard about John he was on his deathbed. They're both really nice, just as nice as you could be. Paul told me he was going with Jane Asher, they weren't sure they would get married or not. I never saw Lennon again. But I saw Paul again because he had Wings; the nice thing that he said about me that I was able to quote was that I was the only older woman that he met that he remembered. How old was he? Probably nineteen, twenty, and I was probably in my thirties or forties. When he came there, I got to meet him with Wings. I met his wife, little kids were running all around and everything. —**Jane Scott**

Jane Scott and I were invited to the press conference and I had my younger brother, who was in high school, come in from Toledo, and he was going to go to the show. I was working at the PD and the press conference was going to be Sunday morning; the show was on Sunday night. That's when that business came out about John Lennon saying they were bigger than Jesus Christ and there was that whole backlash. The word was that the Beatles were not going to have a press conference, so the conference was canceled. So that Sunday morning, my father and mother are in with my brother, staying at my apartment, my father makes us go to church. I get to the concert later that afternoon and Jane Scott tells me, Jeannie, I tried to call you—at the last minute they rescheduled the press conference. This is before cell phones. So Jane went to the press conference and I didn't get a message because we were in church. I said to my father, this is the last time I'm going to church. Didn't do me any good today. —**Jeannie Emser, fan (Bratenahl)**

JANE MISSED THIS ONE:

Ringo ponders while John responds at the Beatles' 1964 news conference in Cleveland.

She was profiled in the *Wall Street Journal*, with the pointillist drawing, and they talked about how she was the world's oldest rock and roll critic. She calls herself the world's oldest teenager because she's older than Dick Clark. After that showed up, apparently she got some calls from people who said, we think this would make a good sitcom, a lady with her young niece, the elderly woman is a rock critic and they find themselves in all these funny concert situations. It never panned out. It's as legitimate an idea as any of the other goofy TV shows that have come and gone. The funny thing is, all these British bands would come into town and say, where's Jane Scott?

And she could disarm anybody. I was at an after-show party for Lou Reed, who usually has a temper and a burr in his saddle. He came into the after-show with a scowl on his face, he was upset about something. He looked around the room; he obviously didn't want to be there. Then he saw Jane Scott, walked over, wrapped his arms around her and kissed her on the cheek, and announced to the crowd that there's two constants to a tour: You play Cleveland and you see Jane Scott. He remembered her because she wrote positive reviews when he played La Cave. He always appreciated that. She could go up and talk to anybody; I saw her do it time and time again. She has this memory that's just astounding, yet in the middle of the conversation she'll think she's talking to somebody else. —**Tom Lash, fan (Cleveland)**

"All these British bands would come into town and say, where's Jane Scott?"

Joan Jett, Akron Civic, might have been about '90 [it was '89], ice storm. In this sea of black leather is a little lady, a little old blond lady in the sensible shoes—and everything was ice—and we recognized her. The guy I was with went over and took her arm and said, "Jane, can we walk you to your car?" She said, "Thank you so much, how'd you like the show?" I saw her a couple of years ago at Westgate Mall. I said, "Hi, Jane," and as I did, somebody else ran up and said, "You're Jane Scott." She just gave her cute little grin. —**Carole Singleton-Chase, fan (North Olmsted)**

Jane would come to the show with her ticket, she would have her safety pin and whatever pass and would put it on her lapel. She'd have her hat on, and a Kodak, and anytime she got backstage she would take food and put it in her purse—she'd always take fruit. Jane's articles were never negative; if she didn't like it, she wouldn't write something bad about it. To her it was always about so and so from Brecksville watching the show; she always mentioned somebody from somewhere. Lyle Lovett, every time Lyle comes to town, he mentions her. —**Barry Gabel, fan (Pepper Pike)**

Jane was powerful. This is how she began her profile of M105 (WWWM-FM) operations manager Eric Stevens for the *Plain Dealer*'s Friday magazine of September 9, 1977:

Notable Northeast Ohio Record Producers and Recording Studios

- After Dark Studios (Parma)
- Agency Recording Studios
- Arnie Rosenberg
- Audio Recording Studios
- Tommy Baker
- Beachwood Studios
- Beat Farm
- Thomas Boddie, Boddie Recording Studio
- Chris Burgess
- Cleveland Recording
- Ken Hamann (mostly an engineer)
- Paul Hamann (mostly an engineer)
- Tommy LiPuma
- Carl Maduri
- Vlad Maleckar
- Joey Miskulin
- Joe Petito (he and Maleckar owned Audio Recording)
- Steve Popovich
- Recording Connection (Beachwood)
- Redda Robbins
- Right Track Studios and Bart Koster
- Suma (Painesville)
- Jimmy Testa
- Don White

He looks like the chubby kid next door. Or a happy college freshman who has just gotten a big CARE package from home.

"Hey, kid, have you seen Mr. Stevens around?" businessmen have been known to ask him."

Bruno Bornino had done a full page on me in the *Cleveland Press.* Two weeks later my promotion director said, "The *Plain Dealer* called—you're going to be on the cover, Jane Scott's doing a feature on you." I said no way. I said, "Call back, make sure it was really the *Plain Dealer.*" And she did, and it was the *Plain Dealer* and it was on the cover of the Friday magazine. The headline was ERIC STEVENS, ROCK RADIO WHIZ KID. And in those days, if you were on the cover, it was the whole cover. It was a three-page piece.
—Eric Stevens, radio executive

Jane Scott, she's just a very kind person, and she loves young guys in bands. She's always been that way. So I grew up with Jane loving the James Gang and Baskerville Hounds or what have you, and when our time came, she wanted to help Johnny Dromette, the Pagans, and Pere Ubu. But she's not really a music critic. You can't read Jane Scott's stuff and understand in any kind of musical terms why you would be interested in this band or another band. She'll just say, "Oh, it's kicky." You're kind of thinking, Jane, you don't understand, the Pagans want to destroy America. But I love Jane.
—John Thompson, fan (Shaker Heights)

Eddie Money and Elvis Costello were playing the Cleveland Agora, this is '77. They were doing a flip tour, where one would open one night, one the other. They get to Cleveland, Eddie's headlining. Elvis goes first and after the Elvis set, Jane stands up, off to the side of the stage, and she's all bent out of shape.

I said, "Jane, what's wrong?"

She says, "I got the wrong color pass, I can't go see Elvis."

I say, "Jane, don't be silly, follow me."

I take Jane past Louie Carter, the security guard backstage that night. I go "Louie, Jane Scott." Louie waves her right in. She walks into the dressing room; there couldn't have been more than six people in the dressing room. Elvis and his manager are catty corner from the side, they see Jane come in, they go, "Out, out, you fat sow. Get out of our dressing room!" They chase her out. I say to Louie, "Somebody's going to pay for this."

The next day, the review comes out in the *Plain Dealer*. Five glowing paragraphs about Eddie Money. Elvis is at the end, he has the sixth para-

Jane stood by Michael Stanley from first to last.

graph and it's not real flattering. For the next week in town, people are going, "Did you see what Jane wrote about Elvis Costello?" —**Peanuts, former band manager**

Elvis Costello and his manager were on somebody's show and they said that we could watch them, but when we came to the show we could not ask them even one word. Without thinking, I said, "How'd it go?" Three little words . . . it had to be a very cheap show because they were cheap. I think it was their manager who made them that way and played up to that quality. I didn't like them. I didn't like the Mentors, but I thought at least they were honest about the way they were. Nobody really cared much about them. —**Jane Scott**

The very first time I got my picture in the paper was in the Friday paper. Jane would do a thing on local bands every week. There was a picture of the Sceptres, taken in my parents' basement—a picture and an article about the band. How great is that? The last night MSB was together, after the final show at the Front Row, it finally hit me that when I walked out of the dressing room that night, MSB was over, that this huge chunk of my life was over. So if I stay in the dressing room, it's still going on. Finally, I was like, face facts, you got to leave. I got my stuff and opened the door, and the only person in the room was Jane. She was waiting. She was right there at the start, she was right there at the end. It made me really smile; if there would be one person in this room, it should be her. And she was there. —**Michael Stanley**

In terms of style and appearance, as well as age, Jane is decades behind her subjects," David Barnett wrote in a feature about Scott (his first) for the November 1978 *Cleveland* magazine. "Despite the trendiness that permeates the rock scene, Jane's personal fashion sense remains skirt-and-blouse or pantssuit conventional, with an occasional dash of the bizarre—such as her proverbial white go-go boots, one of the idiosyncrasies that have made her the butt of affectionate jokes in the music business. But when she speaks, the industry listens. In a town that has become known for new acts, Jane Scott is the one writer anyone in the "biz" *must* talk to. And that's no joke."

MUSIC ON THE MAIN STREAM

Fred Griffith and Wilma Smith, along with *Afternoon Exchange* rock interviewer David Spero, meet Meat Loaf.

PROSPECTING FOR SOUNDS: Record Rendezvous at 300 Prospect was the legendary store run by Leo Mintz and, later, his son Stuart.

SELLING SOUNDS AND STYLES

Retail

The Cleveland rock scene is a patchwork of impressions, and its characters wore many different suits, like Billy Bass, starting his career selling Beatles records at Woolworth's, shifting into radio celebrity, then shaping the market from inside.

> Ward's Folly was the hip place on Coventry. It was a clothing store, late '60s. It was just a little clothing store that would get all the coolest stuff—I remember tie-dye T-shirts, special cool bell-bottoms. Between that and Man Talk, those were the places to find things, unless you went out of town, got on a plane and went up to Yonge Street in Toronto with an empty suitcase. There was a place called Long John's Rock 'n' Roll Clothes—they had the first snakeskin platform boots and crushed velvet pants. I had red, yellow, and kind of an ice blue.
>
> And there was a place in England called Granny Takes a Trip, in London, and there were places all over New York. So if you wanted to be kind of ahead of the trend, you had to be at certain places. There was a fan magazine from England, I think called *Rave,* I have some copies of that somewhere in a crawl space, with pictures of the Small Faces and the Who that would keep you abreast of all that was happening at the time. —**Eric Carmen, musician (Cyrus Erie, the Raspberries, solo)**

ON THE FASHION TIP: Ward's Folly was one of the sources of rock fashion in Cleveland in the '60s.

Ron Clayton managed Man Talk and sold to "many, many, many groups and many progressive individuals—a lot of those musical groups that emanated out of Akron. This is all from '68, '69, '70, '71, '72. At one time, Akron was a big deal, a little prior to the Devo situation."

Among the groups who regularly bought clothes at Man Talk and at the Generation Gap on Coventry, a store Clayton managed earlier, was Grand Funk Railroad. "They appreciated the funkier look that we had at the Generation Gap; we didn't carry any suits," says Clayton, a Cleveland Heights resident.

"They appreciated the funkier look that we had at the Generation Gap; we didn't carry any suits."

Another client was "the Parliaments, that later became Funkadelic—I met every one of those guys, partied with them, all of that, they were from Detroit but for a while they stayed here. They were around all the time, at all the parties and sets around."

> Man Talk was the place where all the new fly stuff used to come in, the colorful stuff. Chuck [Avner, the store owner] and Ron used to look out for us. The funny thing about Man Talk is that [comedian] Steve Harvey, before he made it big any kind of way—this had to be '85, '86—he was in there talking with Chuck. Steve always liked to dress nice, he still dresses nice. He just watched me putting clothes on the counter, and to this day he'll say the first time I met you, you were putting clothes on the counter and I had one coat on layaway. My next gig I'm going to get my coat out. What we liked about Ron is he would take a suit and throw it on the table, and out of nowhere he would find the right shirt and tie and wow, how'd he do that? It was like, okay, I'll take it. —**Gerald Levert, musician**

Fine Threads, Finer Sounds

The British Invasion spurred the growth of record stores. People needed sheet music. They needed 45s.

> The whole British Invasion was my passion, me and about 10 billion other kids. There used to be a very well-known record store, John Wade Records, on Shaker Square. I'd always look for sheet music and things . . . There was a music store downtown in the Old Arcade, I'm trying to remember the name of it—it was there for years and years, on the lower level. During the '60s, they had the sheet music. I was such a Beatles fan, they'd have the words and the music and the chords, it was very exciting for a young person.
>
> Record Rendezvous downtown on Prospect was interesting, too. I used to go to Cuyahoga Community College—the original Tri-C was a collection of old office buildings where Gund Arena now sits. This is '66, '67, and I was still living at home. I would take the Shaker Rapid downtown to Tri-C and I would have to walk from the Terminal Tower up Prospect to Tri-C, going past Record Rendezvous every day. So I stopped in there constantly. It's

very vivid in my head, hearing things playing on the turntables in the record store, like the Byrds and the Band, these different groups they played on their little stereo in the record store. —**Alan Greene, fan (Stow)**

As a high school kid, I had to take the Shaker Rapid downtown once a week to an orthodontist to get my braces tweaked, which gave me an opportunity to 1) stop at Flagg Bros. and ogle the Beatle boots, 2) go up to Higbee's music department and drool over the Vox amplifiers, and 3) stop by Record Rendezvous to get the latest British Invasion LP. I think the prices were $3.19 for mono and $4.19 for stereo, and since I was not rich, all my LPs from that era are mono. In college, the Kent Community Store had a great jazz and blues collection, and believe it or not, Kent's McCrory's had a good one-stop supplying them with bizarre R&B and blues records. Of course, later it was Discodrome on Cedar Hill for punk and new wave.

It was Higbee's Musical Instrument and Record Department. I'd come to the top of the escalator, and there would be a Vox Super Beatle bathed in a blue spotlight—a powerful, heart-stopping icon. My high school band got some "real" Vox gear later from there when our guitarist's parents signed the note.

I would also go to Prospect Music and drool over the guitars and drums but only could afford picks and strings, and drumsticks that I needed for my budget Slingerland set I got at Sodja's. —**Chris Butler, fan (Akron)**

"My high school band got some "real" Vox gear later from Higbee's when our guitarist's parents signed the note."

Downtown stores included Music Grotto, Record Rendezvous, and Discount Records. On the West Side, it was Melody Lane and later, My Generation (both are gone). On the East Side, it was Wax Stacks (long gone) and Record Revolution (still going). For a few years in the late '70s and early '80s, it was Dromes all over the place.

First record I ever sold was *Throw Mama from the Train* by Patti Page. The first hit I had was "Little Darlin'" by the Diamonds; we had two famous promotion men who worked at our branch. One was Carl Maduri, whose son Chris runs some of the radio stations here, and he became famous because he wrote a very famous song, the "Hula Hoop Song," by Georgia Gibbs. The other guy's father was the head of the Palace Theater, Max Mink, and his

Notable Cleveland Record Stores of the 1960s

- Bandstand Records, Maple Hts.
- Disc/Discount Records
- Fantasy Records, Coventry Rd. in Cleveland Hts. (became Record Revolution)
- Melody Lane, Lakewood
- Music Grotto
- Quonset Hut, Akron, Canton, Massillon
- Record Carnival, Great Lakes Mall, Mentor
- Record Rendezvous (over two decades downtown; Richmond Mall, Great Lakes Mall, Randall Mall)
- The Shoppe, Berea
- Tommy Edwards Records
- John Wade Records, Shaker Square
- Halle's, Higbee's, and May Co. each had five branches; and each had a record department.
- Also, In the 1950s and early '60s, you could buy the top-40 singles and some albums at most large drugstores, along with 5- and 10-cent stores like Woolworth's and Kresge's. Discount stores like Giant Tiger, Uncle Bill's, Clarkin's, Zayre's, Spartan Atlantic, Gaylord's, J.P. Snodgrass; and Federal's also carried them.

son, Alan Mink, became our promotion man when we got another branch manager. Wade Whitman became senior branch manager and brought in Alan Mink and was famous for starting the John Wade Record Shop in Shaker Square, a historic record shop.

One of the dealers had this little record shop in Lakewood, Lamp's Melody Lane on Detroit. I ended up buying the store from Walter Lamp on Armistice Day 1946 and sold it on Armistice Day 1964. His best year—this is when albums sold for $3.98, and he sold for full list—was about $50,000. I bought it with a partner who later flaked out, tore down the record booths, and we had the WIXY Top 60 and the Top 200 in *Billboard*. Then we started getting orders for catalogue. The first year of business we did $75,000, and we sold records for $2.98, not $3.98. The grand opening included an artist who had a hit record, Keith. Remember "98.6"?

Record Rendezvous on Prospect was one of my accounts; at nine o'clock in the morning, he [owner Leo Mintz] had an inventory system on yellow cards that would tell you the date he bought, how many he bought, and when it was sold, he'd deduct it. It was a manual inventory system, put in daily, with pencil. So if he bought four on December 1 and on December 5 sold two and you came in a week later, it'd show he was down two. There were thousands of albums to keep track of.

WEST SIDE LANDMARK:

Melody Lane had it all: platters, needles, coupons. Not to mention the trend-setting Daffy Dan and Brad Bell.

Melody Lane was like a bowling alley, and it was narrow. When it was Lamp's Melody Lane it was 15108 Detroit; after I bought the building, I took over the corner store and it became 15100 Detroit, and it became triple size, and that was Melody Lane.

We had windows put in; this is when Daffy Dan joined me at the old store, and Brad Bell, and they were greatly responsible for the youth movement. I was still trying to get them to sell Mantovani. Sometime in the '70s, I opened a store on Chagrin Boulevard in Shaker Heights, called Melody Lane East.

We had Music Grotto by Cleveland State, Pearl Alley and Music Grotto by Ohio State; I had two stores in Columbus. We had two Wax Alley stores, one in Willoughby, one in Southland. We sold candles and records. We're getting into the '80s now. Brad stayed with me all the time. Chuck Murray sold me Music Grotto at Cleveland State and in Columbus. Record Revolution opened up three blocks away from us and couldn't make it either. The kids at Cleveland State are commuters and they don't have time to go shopping.

In the early '80s, the two top stores in Cleveland were Melody Lane on the West Side and Record Revolution on Coventry. Melody Lane was the largest-selling diamond needle store in the whole state. On our bags, they were plastic bags, we printed the top fifteen needles, and we gave them a lifetime guarantee; if you swallowed it, we'd replace it for free, and the prices were unbelievable.

If you burped, I gave you a coupon. If you had bad breath, I gave you a coupon. We sold albums two for $8.98, $9.98; we ended up doing about $350,000 to $400,000 a year, when LPs were $6.98 and $7.98; when the Monkees first came out, we presold them. We took orders: be the first one on your block to have a Monkees album. A dollar deposit, we held the album for you; we sold 250 right off the kicker. Anytime there was a big album, we'd take reservations for them. It was a fun business. —**Shelley Tirk, former record store owner**

"We gave them a lifetime guarantee; if you swallowed it, we'd replace it for free."

I remember the first 45 I ever bought. It was "She Can't Find Her Keys," by Paul Petersen. It's the kind of thing that would appeal to a sixth-grader. A few years later, it was the same thing for people who were buying the Monkees. It was my age group's answer to a Monkees album. In '58, it would have been "Purple People Eater." Another one was Shelley Fabares' "Johnny Angel." I bought them both the same day, at Lamp's Melody Lane, on my way home from school. —**Gail Ghetia Bellamy, fan (Cleveland Heights)**

Daffy Dan fit Melody Lane "like a glove," says Shelley Tirk:

He painted the windows; I about had a heart attack. The mothers wouldn't let the girls go into Melody Lane, because the windows were painted, and Brad Bell, he had platform boots and long hair and spectacles like Elton John and spider rings on every finger and all the parents wouldn't let their kids go into Melody Lane because it was a den of something. Meanwhile, those two really merchandised the store. They were picking the merchandise, they knew what to pick, they knew what albums to buy. I took in waterbeds and they were selling them, and Danny and Brad were building platforms for them. It was becoming more sophisticated. —**Shelley Tirk**

A guy comes into Melody Lane one night, we were open Friday nights until midnight, he wanted this song called "In the Garden of Eden." Brad and I are looking at each other—"In the Garden of Eden?" Finally I said, can you give us some idea how the song goes? The guy goes, "In the garden of

Notable Cleveland Record Stores of the 1970s

Budget Records & Tapes, Lakewood, Cleveland Heights

Disc/Discount Records

Drome, Cleveland Heights, Lakewood, downtown

General Records, Shaker Hts., Maple Hts.

Earwax, Parma

Melody Lane, Lakewood, Shaker Hts., Mayfield Hts.

Music Grotto

Music Madness, Cleveland Hts.

Peaches (key one: at Pearl and Brookpark roads)

Quonset Hut

Record Den, Mentor standalone (formerly in McCrory's Department Store in Great Lakes Mall)

Record Exchange (various East Side locations)

Record Rendezvous

Record Revolution, Coventry Rd. in Cleveland Hts., and Parma (there was one at E. 20th and Euclid in the early '70s)

Record Theatre (various locations)

Shattered Records, Lakewood

The Shoppe, Berea

Sound Of Music, Brunswick

Swampwood Records, Lakewood

IN THE GROTTO:
Billy Bass explains psychedelic style to a customer at the Music Grotto.

Eden, baby." I think we fell out laughing behind the counter. We had great speakers and a sound system inside the Melody Lane in Lakewood and this big armchair we had mounted on top of a Pepsi machine. I used to sit in this armchair to watch the record store, watch the people, get into what was going on. The store was like 15 feet by 70 feet . . . I had gotten from a billboard company a WNCR billboard, a good-sized one, and had stapled this to the ceiling. We built a canopy over the counter with a roof on it and stapled 45s on it as shingles. We sold waterbeds in there later on, too. —**Dan Gray, owner of "Daffy Dan's"**

Shelley Tirk calls Music Grotto a disaster. Billy Bass recalls it differently:

It was across the street from Cleveland State University on 24th and Euclid, and Chuck figured all we got to do was put some record racks in there, the college kids will just come over. So that's what we did; nobody came over. It was not a destination place, and the college kids weren't coming over to buy records. Nobody was coming except a hippie couple named Jack Novosel and his girlfriend Chad. The very first thing they said to me was "Far out, man." That was the first time I heard that expression. I'm looking at them—what? They looked like if Madison Avenue said, here's what hippies looked like in the '60s. They wore bell-bottoms; he looked like a young, hip Sonny and she looked like a young, hip Cher. They said, we can fix this place up, we can make this place look like something. I said okay, go ahead.

And that's when they painted the place psychedelic and fluorescent colors, and once we had the psychedelic weirdness look, then I added the love beads that were popular back in those days, the peace symbol, the black light posters, and most importantly, the music that was not popular. If people came downtown to buy records, they'd go to Disc Records, where Martin Perlich worked, or Record Rendezvous, which had been established for twenty years. I had to be different. If it had a psychedelic album cover, chances are the record would sell. And then they'd hear it and maybe like it. Sometimes it worked, sometimes it didn't. When it was Jimi Hendrix or Cream or Grateful Dead or Jefferson Airplane or Steve Miller, it worked. Or Canned Heat or the Doors. Sometimes it was Ultimate Spinach, groups like that, and it didn't work. One thing for sure: if you wanted the new sound or rock and roll, the place to come and get it was Music Grotto. —**Billy Bass, DJ, former record store manager**

"If it had a psychedelic album cover, chances are the record would sell. And then they'd hear it and maybe like it."

DOWNTOWN MECCA:

The psychedelic ruled at Music Grotto, in the ambience and, above all, in the albums that played there. This old ad hints at the vibe.

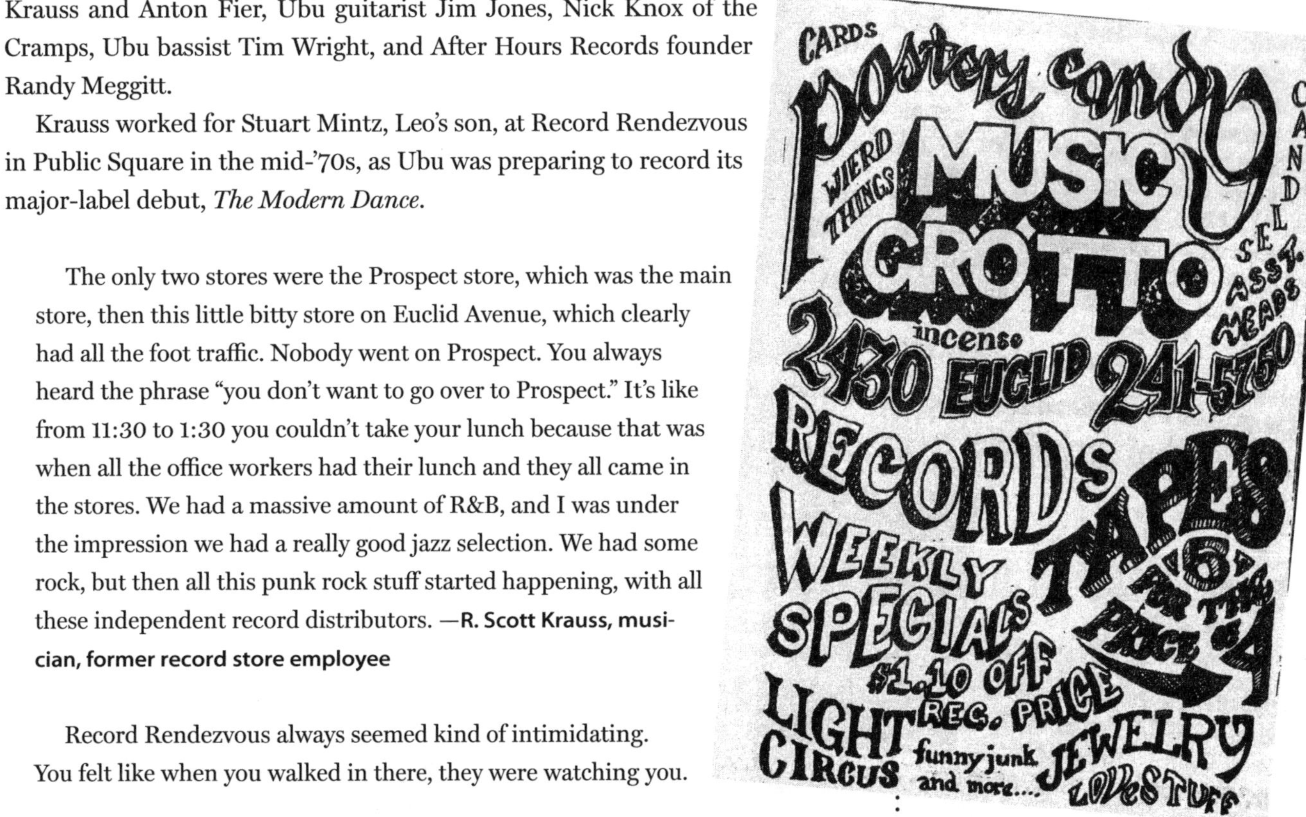

Much of Cleveland's underground matriculated at Record Rendezvous at 300 Prospect. Those who worked there included Pere Ubu drummers R. Scott Krauss and Anton Fier, Ubu guitarist Jim Jones, Nick Knox of the Cramps, Ubu bassist Tim Wright, and After Hours Records founder Randy Meggitt.

Krauss worked for Stuart Mintz, Leo's son, at Record Rendezvous in Public Square in the mid-'70s, as Ubu was preparing to record its major-label debut, *The Modern Dance*.

The only two stores were the Prospect store, which was the main store, then this little bitty store on Euclid Avenue, which clearly had all the foot traffic. Nobody went on Prospect. You always heard the phrase "you don't want to go over to Prospect." It's like from 11:30 to 1:30 you couldn't take your lunch because that was when all the office workers had their lunch and they all came in the stores. We had a massive amount of R&B, and I was under the impression we had a really good jazz selection. We had some rock, but then all this punk rock stuff started happening, with all these independent record distributors. —**R. Scott Krauss, musician, former record store employee**

Record Rendezvous always seemed kind of intimidating. You felt like when you walked in there, they were watching you.

Songs that Refer to Cleveland

"Anything but Mine" - Kenny Chesney
"Bad Bad Cleveland Browns" - Cleveland Beat
"Born Too Late" - Poni-Tails
"Boy Next Door" - The Secrets
"Burn On" - Randy Newman
"Cleveland Calling" - Chris Rea
"Cleveland Is the City" - Bone Thugs N Harmony
"Cleveland Love Song" - KYW Singers
"Cleveland Park" - Edwin McCain
"Cleveland Rocks" - Ian Hunter
"Cleveland Shuffle" - I-71 North
"Cleveland" - Jewel
"Get Your Ass to Cleveland" - Pat Dailey
"Go All the Way" - Raspberries
"High School USA" (Cleveland version) - Tommy Facenda
"It's All the Same" - James Gang
"Kissin' Time" - Bobby Rydell or Kiss
"Let's Move to Cleveland" - Frank Zappa
"Little Bit O' Soul" - The Music Explosion
"Look Out Cleveland" - The Band
"Ohio (Come Back to Texas)" - Bowling for Soup
"Old Friend" - Rancid
"Pancho and Lefty" - Willie Nelson

But there was another record store, I can't think of the name of it, on Euclid at Ontario. It was a tiny little store. That's where I did my record shopping. This other place, it was small, easy to find what you needed, they were always playing great music in there. But it wasn't a place where you'd go for unusual stuff. It was there for years and years and years. Morrow's Nuts used to be next door.

When I was a kid, my buddy and I used to come downtown a lot. You'd go to Higbee's, get a Frostie, go to Park Lunch. And we'd go to the record store. It was a place to hang out. It wasn't avant-garde at all, but it was the place to get the new Beatles single. They had sheet music when you walked in the door. —**Ed Watkins, fan (North Olmsted)**

Prospect was tough back then. One night I was walking home on Prospect—there's a church at the corner of 30th and Prospect next to the Cadillac dealership. It was cold and I was walking home, tired. There was a gym down the street, like at 22nd, I was just coming home from the gym. There was a guy lying on the steps of the church with a hole in his forehead, like a big ruby. It was intense, man. —**Tony Maimone, fan (Brooklyn, N.Y.)**

We would sit behind an iron fence in front of the building [the Plaza at 32nd and Prospect] when clubs were closing, and there was a lot of prostitution on the street, and every now and then, they'd do stings with the decoys, the copstitutes—I just made that word up there. So we would sit there with a case of beer and watch the copstitutes and the soon-to-be-jailed johns do business. Basically, a woman would lean into a window and start talking to the guy. You couldn't hear what they were saying, but a few minutes later cops would swarm in. —**Larry Collins, fan (Cleveland)**

One alternative to Prospect (and to downtown record stores) was the Drome, a succession of record stores in Cleveland Heights, downtown, and Lakewood.

My idea with the Drome was to say, look, everybody, we got a lot of talent here, and we don't need the national corporations to tell us what's cool and

what we should do. When I lived in L.A., we knew lots of people in bands, and whenever they talked about their music, they were always trying to describe what they did in terms of sort of handles, like we're kind of like Guns N' Roses meets whatever, always trying to anticipate what the A&R guys were looking for. Whereas here in Cleveland, you first of all would never think anybody was ever going to come from L.A. and sign you anyway. You would play the music you were going to anyway and do it from your heart as you saw it. —**John Thompson [Johnny Dromette], former record store owner**

The first Drome, Hideo's Discodrome, opened in June 1976 at Cedar and Fairmount.

He would have Devo and bands like that playing, he was getting all kinds of imports from England, when you could find stuff like the Clash, Chris Spedding, the Sex Pistols, the whole punk thing, as well as New York Dolls, Cramps, the Ramones, Blondie, Richard Hell. From there, he went to right below the Phantasy; I remember seeing Patti Smith in there reading poetry, she autographed one of her first books of poetry for me. That would have been, like, not too long after *Horses* came out; I remember seeing her at the Agora when that album came out—this might have been '76, '77. Then he was up on Huron, the Huron-Prospect Triangle. He kind of knew what I liked; he'd tell me, I've got some new Roxy stuff; he turned me on to the first Psychedelic Furs record. And he always did the covers for the Ubu records. **—Chris Jacobs, fan (Rocky River)**

In 1978, the landlord disapproved of a couple of things we were doing in there—we were having these Sunday shows in the store, we had Devo in there one weekend. We had the Dead Boys posing naked in the window, traffic going by, they were pulling their pants down and pulling that trick where you pull your dick back behind your legs so it looks like you're a girl. It wasn't planned, it was just like, oh, we'll do a publicity stunt here in the window.

"The landlord felt we were bringing a bad element to the neighborhood."

It happened very fast so no one really took note, but the landlord heard about it and he just felt we were bringing a bad element to the neighborhood, so the lawyer for the landlord said, we will give you a month's free rent

"Precious" - the Pretenders
"Regeneration" - Stone Temple Pilots
"Rhythm of the Rain" - Cascades, John Gummoe
"Sheraton Gibson" - Pete Townshend.
"SOS" - Edwin Starr
"Stairway to Cleveland" - Jefferson Starship
"The Heart of Rock & Roll" - Huey Lewis & the News
"There's No Surf in Cleveland" - Euclid Beach Band
"Time Won't Let Me" - Outsiders
"Wreck of the Edmund Fitzgerald" - Gordon Lightfoot

Contributions by: Mike Norman, Plain Dealer Arts Editor; Tom Feran, Plain Dealer Columnist; John Soeder, Plain Dealer pop music critic; Chuck Benjamin, radio historian

Notable Cleveland Record Stores of the 1980s

Chris's Warped Records, Lakewood
Disc Connection, Parma
Drome
Harmony Lane
My Generation, Westlake
Peaches
Platterpuss, Euclid
Recordland (a national chain with numerous local outlets)
Record Revolution
Record Theatre / Repeat the Beat
Royal Garden Records, North Olmsted
Shattered Records
The Shoppe, Berea
Sound Of Music
Wax Stacks, Cleveland Hts.

and forgive the month you're behind and you can tear up the lease. Michael Weldon had started working there, and he's from Lakewood, so he was all excited: Let's go over to the West Side. I was always curious about the West Side and thought the schism between the East and West Side was ridiculous. We kind of got paid to leave—we went to the West Side, and my reflection over the long haul is yes, it is different over there. That's why I live on the East Side. —**John Thompson**

In Lakewood there was the Phantasy, the Drome had their store there. There was the Real World across the street, it was Hennessy's after the Real World, and Johnny Dromette would have the Pagans play in the store sometimes. In Lakewood, which was gestapoland as far as authority, I remember, I think it was Mike Hudson of the Pagans was drinking a gallon of whiskey out on the street. They would just hang out on the street and drink and the Pagans would play punk rock and there would be like seven people in the audience because they weren't popular. And the cops would leave us alone. I think the cops were cool, considering they were Lakewood and it was punk back when it had such a bad name. —**Marie Vivolo, fan (Cleveland)**

You would walk in there and not know 90 percent of what was in the bins, particularly when the punk rock thing happened and Johnny Dromette opened the Drome in Lakewood. I used to go into the store and shop, and here's this guy with eye makeup on, real long straight hair with a girl's clip in the back, very anti-establishment, doing his own thing, opened this record store and literally had all the punk releases from across the country. And he would promote shows down at the Agora, with the Pagans and Pere Ubu. —**Tom Lash, fan (Cleveland)**

"You would walk in there and not know 90 percent of what was in the bins, particularly when the punk rock thing happened."

We did a year and a half in Lakewood, I think, and that was a point at which I fired everybody that worked there. That was partly because I was fucked up myself, but the whole thing was financially untenable and I knew I could talk my dad into loaning me enough money to revive the store one more time, and that was in the Point Building, 1290 Euclid, a little triangular building attached to the end of Halle's. The goal downtown was simply to pay the cheapest rent possible, try to achieve profitability week after

week—and actually, when we were downtown it was profitable two weeks out of three—then liquidate the inventory and figure out something else to do with my life. I had gotten really just fed up.

I brought *Eraserhead* to Cleveland years before it appeared in any revival theater, and I got an audience of five people a night for the week I played it. I did booking for Pirate's Cove, we also booked the Phantasy nightclub in Lakewood. That was the appeal of Lakewood for us, because in the building was the Homestead Theater and the Phantasy. I think we did Magazine in there, we did the Real Kids from Boston, and B52s—we did a show in the Homestead Theater with them and also promoted them at the Governor's Chateau on West 117th south of Lorain. Probably '79. —**John Thompson**

One time me and a girlfriend went to the Drome between Euclid and Huron and we were both tripping and there was a back window that went onto Huron, where there was an outside mall and there was a party in the park in the mall. They used to do it every Friday. There'd be a band, and people would sit around and drink a lot of beer and unwind from the week. I remember we started putting on puppet shows in the window. We were, like, these punks and the people there were, like, your—what would you call them—preppies. Office workers, that kind of thing. We went into the basement of the Drome, tried to find some props. Myself and my girlfriend at the time and, I think, John and his girlfriend at the time were just kind of having a laugh at our expense. It ended up where they taped us to the window. I was much thinner, so a plate glass window could hold me. We were tripping so I really don't know what was going on. We were having so much fun we weren't paying attention to the people we were supposed to be entertaining. —**Larry Collins, fan (Cleveland)**

PHOTO CREDITS

Frequently cited sources are referred to by the codes listed below. All other sources are cited with full name.

Auth: Author's collection
Burford: Courtesy of Bob Burford
CSU: Cleveland Press Collection, Cleveland State University Archives
CPL: Cleveland Public Library
Gray: Courtesy of Dan Gray
Macoska: Photo by Janet Macoska
Macoska*: Courtesy of Janet Macoska
Scene: Courtesy of Scene Magazine and Don Kriss

Various concert tickets courtesy of Bob Burford, Jack Caine, Patty Duber, Dan Gray, and Jim Henke.

FOREWORD p. 4 Gray

RADIO p. 6 Macoska*; p. 7 courtesy of Ruth Fisher Freed and www.alanfreed.com; p. 8 (left) courtesy of Ruth Fisher Freed and www.alanfreed.com; p. 8 (right) photo by Peter Hastings courtesy of Holly Hastings; p. 9 (top and bottom) Macoska*; p. 10 (top) Macoska*; p. 10 (bottom) courtesy of Pat Randle; p. 11 (top) courtesy of David Barnett; p. 11 (bottom) Macoska*; p. 12 (top and bottom) Macoska*; p. 13 (top and middle) Macoska*; p. 13 (bottom) Burford; p. 14 (top) Burford; p. 14 (bottom) photo by George Shuba; p. 15 courtesy of Martin Perlich; p. 16 courtesy of Billy Bass; p. 18 courtesy of Billy Bass; p. 19 (top) courtesy of Denny Sanders; p. 19 (bottom) courtesy of Gary Pearlman; p. 20 Gray; p. 21 (top) Macoska*; p. 21 (bottom) Scene; p. 22 Gray; p. 23 Scene

THE BRITISH INVADE p. 24 photo by George Shuba; p. 26 (left) courtesy of Gail Ghetia Bellamy; p. 26 (right) photo by George Shuba; p. 27 Burford; p. 31 courtesy of Jim Henke; p. 32 Macoska; p. 33 photo by George Shuba; p. 34 courtesy of Jim Henke; p. 35 (top) Macoska; p. 35 (top) courtesy of Jim Henke

NATIONAL ACTS p. 40 courtesy of Larry Bruner; p. 41 (left) courtesy of Larry Bruner; p. 41 (right) photo by George Shuba; p. 43 Macoska; p. 44 Macoska; p. 45 Macoska; p. 46 CSU; p. 47 photo by David Spero; p. 48 Burford; p. 49 (top) photo by David Spero; p. 49 (left and bottom) Burford; p. 50 Scene; p. 51 Macoska; p. 52 courtesy of Hank LoConti; p. 53 Macoska

LOCAL LEGENDS p. 54 (top and bottom) CSU; p. 55 Auth; p. 56 (top) courtesy of Eudi Tracy; p. 56 (bottom) Auth; p. 57 courtesy of Buddy Maver; p. 58 (top) photo by Leo Smith courtesy of Sue Schmidt-Horning and Deb Smith; p. 58 (bottom) courtesy of Sue Schmidt-Horning and Deb Smith; p. 59 (top right) Auth; p. 59 (top left) courtesy of Richard Greene; p. 59 (bottom) courtesy of Sam Gabel; p. 60 (top) Auth; p. 60 (bottom) Gray; p. 61 (top left and bottom) Gray; p. 61 (top right) courtesy of Frank Musarra; p. 62 Gray; p. 63 (top) courtesy of Hank LoConti; p. 63 (bottom) Auth; p. 64 (top) Auth; p. 64 (bottom) Macoska; p. 65 (top) Macoska; p. 65 (bottom) Auth; p. 66 (top) Gray; p. 66 (bottom) courtesy of David Spero; p. 67 (left) Scene; p. 67 (right) Auth

OTHER LOCAL ACTS p. 68 courtesy of Robert Kidney; p. 69 Auth; p. 71 courtesy of Dale Flanigan; p. 72 (top) Macoska; p. 72 (middle) Burford; p. 72 (bottom) courtesy of Rob Lucas; p. 73 (top and bottom) Macoska; p. 74 courtesy of Marie Vivolo; p. 75 Macoska; p. 76 Macoska; p. 77 courtesy of Robert Kidney; p. 78 (left) courtesy of Marie Vivolo; p. 78 (right) courtesy of Robert Kidney; p. 79 (top) Auth; p. 79 (bottom) courtesy of Marie Vivolo; p. 80 Burford; p. 81 Auth; p. 82 courtesy of Alan Greene; p. 85 Scene

CLUBS p. 86 Macoska; p. 88 Auth; p. 89 (top and bottom) Gray; p. 90 CPL; p. 91 (top) Macoska; p. 91 (bottom) Auth; p. 92 (left) Macoska; p. 92 (right) courtesy of Buddy Maver; p. 93 (top) Scene; p. 93 (middle) courtesy of Hank LoConti; p. 93 (bottom) Macoska; p. 94 Macoska; p. 95 (top right) Auth; p. 95 (middle) Scene; p. 95 (bottom left) CPL; p. 99 (top) courtesy of Larry Bruner; p. 99 (bottom) courtesy of Mac's Backs; p. 102 Auth; p. 103 (top) CSU; p. 103 (bottom) courtesy of Mike Belkin

MUSIC AND THE MEDIA p. 104 courtesy of Sam Gabel; p. 105 courtesy of David Spero; p. 106 courtesy of David Spero; p. 107 (top) photo by Harry Spero, courtesy of David Spero; p. 107 (bottom) CSU; p. 108 courtesy of Jim Henke; p. 109 CSU; p. 110 courtesy of Billy Bass; p. 111 Macoska; p. 112 Macoska; p. 113 photo by David Spero; p. 115 Author's collection; p. 116 Macoska; p. 117 courtesy of David Spero

RETAIL p. 118 Macoska*; p. 119 courtesy of Mac's Backs; p. 120 Scene; p. 121 Scene; p. 122 (top) Auth; p. 122 (second and bottom) courtesy of Shelley Tirk; p. 122 (third) courtesy of Gail Ghetia Bellamy; p. 124 (left) Scene; p. 124 (right) CPL; p. 125 (top) CPL; p. 125 (bottom) Mac's Backs p. 126 Scene; p. 127 CSU; p. 128 (top) courtesy of Marie Vivolo; p. 128 (bottom) Scene; p. 129 Scene

ACKNOWLEDGMENTS

I want to thank the following people who shared their memories, knowledge, household and bandwidth to help me produce this book. I could not include all their memories, but their input gave shape, melody and, hopefully, rhythm to this enterprise. Here are the members of my book's band: Mark Addison, Bill Anderson, Andrew Axilrod, John Awarski, David Barnett, Dennis Barrie, Billy Bass, Greg Beaumont, Hal Becker, Jules Belkin, Mike Belkin, Michael Belkin, Brad Bell, Steve Bellamy, Chuck Benjamin, Lynn "Pierre" Bennett, Larry Bole, Ruthie Brown, Sherrod Brown, Larry Bruner, Wally Bryson, David Budin, Bob Burford, Chris Butler, Lyn Byrd, Jack Caine, Denny Carleton, Eric Carmen, Rick Christyson, Ron Clayton, Marc Cohn, Larry Collins, Dan Cook, Joe DeFazio, Suzanne DeGaetano, Chuy De Los Santos, Laura DeMarco, Evan DeWitt, Michael Dreyfuss, Patty Duber, Art Dussault, Colin Dussault, Frank Dutton, Jeannie Emser, Jim Eng, Tom Feran, Dale Flanigan, Dewey Forward, Frank Foti, Jimmy Fox, Barry and Sam Gabel, Sonny Geraci, George Ghetia, Ray Glasser, Dick Goddard, Carl Gonzalez, John Gorman, Dan Gray, Richard Green, Alan Greene, Joyce Halasa, Michael Heaton, Jim Henke, Bruce Hennes, Norm Isaac, Chris Jacobs, Jan Kallay, Bob Keesecker, Jack and Bob Kidney, Bart Koster, R. Scott Krauss, Don Kriss, Ernie Krivda, Jill Kuhn, Howard Landau, Matt "the Cat" Lapczynski, Tom Lash, John Lenear (died July 14, 2006), Rob Levandoski, Eddie Levert, Gerald Levert, Gary Lippe, Hank LoConti, Janet Macoska, Joe Madigan, Jeff Magnum, Tony Maimone, Vince Malatesta, Ken Margolis, Joe Matuscak, Buddy Maver, Matt McManus, Bill "Mr. Stress" Miller, Larry Morrow, Frank Musarra, Tami Nato, Paul Nickels, Michael Norman, Eric Olsen, Mike Olszewski, Clay Pasternak, Peanuts, Gary Pearlman, Harvey Pekar, Martin Perlich, John Petkovic, Jason Pettigrew, Michael Pierson, Steve Popovich, Steve Presser, Jim Quinn, Chuck Rambaldo, Pat Randle, Nancy Reese, Mitch Renko, Mark Ribbins, Denny Sanders, Mike Sanson, Jane Scott, Rich Spina, Sue Schmidt-Horning, Don Sebian, Patty Sheehan, George Shuba, Carole Singleton-Chase, George Sipl, Deb Smith, Sandy Smith, John Soeder, David Spero, Rich Spina, George Stage, Michael Stanley, Eric Stevens, Quinn Stilletto, Bill Strawbridge, Harold Sudberry, Dave Swanson, John Thompson, Shelley Tirk, Norm Tischler, Pete Tokar, Eudi Tracey, Lawrence "Kid Leo" Travagliante, Sue Vendetti, Marie Vivolo, Norman Wain, Ed Watkins, Don Webster, and Chris Wright. I particularly want to tip my hat to Gail Ghetia Bellamy, whose encouragement and advice proved invaluable in moments (and there were several) of stress. So much love and so much more than acknowledgment go to my wife and favorite editor, Karen Sandstrom, and my children, Lylah Rose Sandstrom Wolff and Katy Nozar. Their affection and patience kept my crankiness at bay and my creativity on track.

More Cleveland Memories . . .

Cleveland Summertime Memories
by Gail Ghetia Bellamy

What made summer special growing up in Cleveland? Taking a dip at the city pool with your best friends. Building a sandcastle in your clam diggers at Edgewater Park. Pulling up to Manners Big Boy in your parents' car for a burger and a Big Ghoulardi. Watching the Indians lose (again) but being dazzled by the fireworks at Municipal Stadium. Riding the Rocket Ship and then being terrified by Laughing Sal at Euclid Beach Park. Packing a picnic for the first season at Blossom.

Enjoy stories told by dozens of Northeast Ohioians who shared in the same fun and excitement of growing up here.

Paperback / 126 pages / 256 photos

Cleveland Christmas Memories
by Gail Ghetia Bellamy

What made Christmas extra-special to a Cleveland kid? Come relive some of your fondest moments . . .

Seeing Mr. Jingeling (the keeper of Santa's keys) on TV or in person at Halle's. Gazing at the giant Sterling-Lindner tree. Ice skating on Public Square. The brilliant holiday lighting display at GE's Nela Park . . .

Join in as dozens of Northeast Ohioans share their personal stories of Christmas past; includes recollections of people who made Christmas happen, too: former Santas, retail window dressers, entertainers, and of course parents.

Paperback / 126 pages / 234 photos

Cleveland Food Memories
by Gail Ghetia Bellamy

Remember when food was local? Cleveland companies made it, and local people sold it and ran the restaurants where we ate it. Now, take a delicious trip into the past.

Food makes powerful memories. Mention Hough Bakery and see how quickly we Clevelanders start to drool over just the thought of those long-lost white cakes. This book collects the fondest memories of Clevelanders who still ache for treats from the past. There were Frostees in the Higbee's basement. Popcorn balls at Euclid Beach. Burgers at Manner's or Mawby's. Entertainment-filled nights at Alpine Village. Mustard at old Municipal Stadium . . . and so much more.

Paperback / 112 pages / 209 photos

Cleveland Amusement Park Memories
by David and Diane Francis

Northeast Ohioans who grew up visiting amusement parks in the 1940s through 1970s will cherish these memories of Euclid Beach Park, Luna Park, Geauga Lake Park, Puritas Springs Park, White City, Memphis Kiddie Park, Geneva-on-the-Lake, and others.

Each park had its own personality, its own alluring smells and sounds. At Euclid Beach it was the stately sycamores and the unforgettable odor of the lake and of damp earth beneath the pier. At Puritas Springs, the odor of warm oil on the chain of the Cyclone coaster. The chatter of Monkey Island at Luna Park, the sharp reports of the Shooting Gallery at Geauga Lake.

Paperback / 128 pages / 192 photos

More information and samples at: **www.grayco.com**